Literary Lives

General Editor: **Richard Dutton**, Professor of English, Lancaster University

This series offers stimulating accounts of the literary careers of the most admired and influential English-language authors. Volumes follow the outline of the writers' working lives, not in the spirit of traditional biography, but aiming to trace the professional, publishing and social contexts which shaped their writing.

Published titles include:

Clinton Machann
MATTHEW ARNOLD

Jan Fergus
JANE AUSTEN

Tom Winnifrith and Edward Chitham
CHARLOTTE AND EMILY BRONTË

Sarah Wood
ROBERT BROWNING

Janice Farrar Thaddeus
FRANCES BURNEY

Caroline Franklin
BYRON

Nancy A. Walker
KATE CHOPIN

Roger Sales
JOHN CLARE

Cedric Watts
JOSEPH CONRAD

Grahame Smith
CHARLES DICKENS

George Parfitt
JOHN DONNE

Paul Hammond
JOHN DRYDEN

Kerry McSweeney
GEORGE ELIOT

Tony Sharpe
T.S. ELIOT

Harold Pagliaro
HENRY FIELDING

Andrew Hook
F. SCOTT FITZGERALD

Mary Lago
E.M. FORSTER

Shirley Foster
ELIZABETH GASKELL

Neil Sinyard
GRAHAM GREENE

James Gibson
THOMAS HARDY

Gerald Roberts
GERARD MANLEY HOPKINS

Kenneth Graham
HENRY JAMES

W. David Kaye
BEN JONSON

Phillip Mallett
RUDYARD KIPLING

John Worthen
D.H. LAWRENCE

Angela Smith
KATHERINE MANSFIELD

Lisa Hopkins
CHRISTOPHER MARLOWE

Cedric C. Brown
JOHN MILTON

Peter Davison
GEORGE ORWELL

Linda Wagner-Martin
SYLVIA PLATH

Felicity Rosslyn
ALEXANDER POPE

Richard Dutton
WILLIAM SHAKESPEARE

John Williams
MARY SHELLEY

Michael O'Neill
PERCY BYSSHE SHELLEY

Gary Waller
EDMUND SPENSER

Tony Sharpe
WALLACE STEVENS

Joseph McMinn
JONATHAN SWIFT

Leonée Ormond
ALFRED TENNYSON

Peter Shillingsburg
WILLIAM MAKEPEACE THACKERAY

David Wykes
EVELYN WAUGH

John Mepham
VIRGINIA WOOLF

John Williams
WILLIAM WORDSWORTH

Alasdair D.F. Macrae
W.B. YEATS

Literary Lives
Series Standing Order ISBN 0–333–71486–5 hardcover
Series Standing Order ISBN 0–333–80334–5 paperback
(*outside North America only*)

You can receive future titles in this series as they are published by placing a standing order. Please contact your bookseller or, in case of difficulty, write to us at the address below with your name and address, the title of the series and one of the ISBNs quoted above.

Customer Services Department, Macmillan Distribution Ltd, Houndmills, Basingstoke, Hampshire RG21 6XS, England

---

Graham Greene

A Literary Life

Neil Sinyard

First published 2003 by
PALGRAVE MACMILLAN
Houndmills, Basingstoke, Hampshire RG21 6XS and
175 Fifth Avenue, New York, N.Y. 10010
Companies and representatives throughout the world

PALGRAVE MACMILLAN is the global academic imprint of the Palgrave Macmillan division of St. Martin's Press, LLC and of Palgrave Macmillan Ltd. Macmillan® is a registered trademark in the United States, United Kingdom and other countries. Palgrave is a registered trademark in the European Union and other countries.

ISBN 0–333–72986–2 hardback
ISBN 0–333–72987–0 paperback

This book is printed on paper suitable for recycling and made from fully managed and sustained forest sources.

A catalogue record for this book is available from the British Library.

Library of Congress Cataloging-in-Publication Data
Sinyard, Neil.
   Graham Greene: a literary life / Neil Sinyard.
      p.   cm. — (Literary lives)
   Filmography: p.
   Includes bibliographical references (p.) and index.
   ISBN 0–333–72986–2
   1. Greene, Graham, 1904–1991.   2. Novelists, English—20th century—Biography.   3. Screenwriters—Great Britain—Biography.   I. Title.   II. Literary lives (New York, N.Y.)

   PR6013.R44Z847 2003
   823'.912—dc21   2003053572

10   9   8   7   6   5   4   3   2   1
12   11   10   09   08   07   06   05   04   03

Printed and bound in Great Britain by
Antony Rowe Ltd, Chippenham and Eastbourne

Contents

Acknowledgements

In a letter to J.A. Symons in the Spring of 1886, Robert Louis Stevenson recounted the shattering impact on him of reading Dostoevsky's *Crime and Punishment*. 'It was like having an illness,' he said. 'Some find it dull; Henry James couldn't finish it; all I can say is, it nearly finished me.'

Writing this book has been something like that. I finished it; it nearly finished me. Every physical, psychological, methodological, mechanical thing that could go wrong did go wrong, whether it took the form of computer virus, printer breakdown, inexplicable deletion or disappearance of files, an embargo on primary research material that made it impossible to take advantage of a generous research grant, or a mysterious illness that developed into a morbid agoraphobia, undoubtedly the least helpful malady to contract when researching the most globe-trotting major author in history. I have written over twenty books and I mention this only in order to say, with feeling, that this one has been more trouble than all of the others put together. It is nevertheless still intended, to use Greene terminology, as 'an entertainment'. I have even endeavoured to make the footnotes entertaining. This is not going to be one of those biographies that, to paraphrase D.J. Taylor on the recent book about Anthony Burgess by Roger Lewis (*The Guardian*, 8 November 2002), becomes an extended diary about the biographer's problems with his subject and the problems connected with the subject of biography. This introduction is simply to provide the context for the following list of people, to whom I wish to express my deep gratitude: without their inspiration and encouragement, direct or indirect, this book could never have been written.

Chief amongst these are the members of the Graham Greene Birthplace Trust, with whom I have had close links since its foundation in 1998. Connection with the Trust has enabled me to have the privilege of meeting members of Greene's family, including his daughter Caroline Bourget and his nephew Nicholas Dennys, who have been particularly gracious. Also the annual Greene Festival in Berkhamsted, which the Trust organises and which takes place around the time of

Greene's birthday, has brought me into contact with some of the very finest scholars, directors and interpreters of Greene's work, including (in alphabetical order) Judith Adamson, Martin Corner, Maria Couto, Peter Duffell, Leopoldo Duran, Quentin Falk, Bryan Forbes, Philip French, Christopher Hampton, Ian Hart, Giles Havergal, Maire McQueeney, Michael Meyer, Anthony Mockler, Norman Sherry, Martin Stannard, Cedric Watts and Stephen Woolley. This is by no means a definitive list of the distinguished speakers who have attended the Festival: these are simply the ones whose ideas I have had the good fortune to hear and/or discuss at this event, and I thank them all for the stimulus their thoughts have given me. My particular thanks, though, go to the organisers whose hospitality towards me has developed into lasting friendship: Roger and Joan Watkins, David and Liz Pearce, Ken and Jenny Sherwood. This book is affectionately dedicated to them, with an additional vote of thanks to all the members of the Trust who have shown me such kindness on my annual pilgrimage there. It used to be said of Leonard Bernstein that, when he got tired of American and British critics sniping at him, he would retire to Vienna where he knew he was assured of a warm welcome. For me it's Berkhamsted. Considering his own view of the place, Graham Greene might have been intrigued and amused by that.

I owe special thanks also to Ken Annakin, for talking to me of his experience of working with Greene on the film, *Loser Takes All* (1955); to Yan Christensen, for entrusting me to be the literary editor of the Greene Newsletter and for numerous acts of generosity, including a gift of a resplendent poster for the 1957 film of *The Quiet American*; and to Peter Duffell, for his courteous correspondence and the loan of his fascinating first screenplay for *The Honorary Consul* (1973), before the project was assigned elsewhere. Richard Dutton gently coaxed me into doing this book and has been the most patient of Series' editors. The British Academy generously lent its support to this project. My colleagues at Hull University have been unfailingly supportive as always, and I have benefited particularly (in ways they may not always have sensed) from astute comments by James Booth, Angela Leighton, Rowlie Wymer and my much missed friend, the late Gillian West. My indispensable co-teacher in the Film Studies section, Melanie Williams has been a precious source of sympathetic and constructive advice. Ruth Green has always been unstinting with valuable secretarial assistance. Above all, my brilliant family – my wife Lesley, and children Nathalie, Jessica and Joel – have done more than just cope with the turmoil of having to live with a Greene biographer (one of the most stressful of all domestic situations), and have done more than just provide the kind of loving environment that facilitates the writer's task in keeping life's priorities in perspective. At crucial stages in this narrative, they have solved seemingly impossible information technology problems that have baffled and defeated the experts, and on occasions they have even retrieved the irretrievable. In other words, they are not only compassion incarnate but computer literate as well: you cannot ask more of a family than that.

Every effort has been made by the author and publishers to secure permissions for all relevant works, and if any have been missed we will be happy to rectify the situation at the earliest opportunity.

The Greene Chronology: Some Major Dates and Events

1904–20

Henry Graham Greene is born on 2 October 1904 in Berkhamsted, Hertfordshire. Among his first words are 'Poor dog', a reference to his sister's dead pug that had been run over by a carriage and carried home lying at baby Graham's feet in his pram. He is the son of Charles Henry Greene, later to become headmaster of Berkhamsted school (1910–27), and Marion Raymond Greene, first cousin of one of Greene's early literary heroes, Robert Louis Stevenson. Greene himself is the cousin of another of the century's major writers, Christopher Isherwood.

He is the fourth of six children, and the third of four boys who will grow into very tall men. His younger brother is Hugh, to whom he is very close and who will achieve eminence as the director-general of the BBC (1960–69). His elder brother is Raymond, his father's favourite, school prefect and Head of House, who will go on to become a distinguished doctor. His eldest brother is Herbert – according to Graham, the black sheep of the family and who is the model for the feckless and irresolute Anthony Farrant character in *England Made Me* (1935).

Key event

At the age of fourteen, he becomes a boarder at Berkhamsted School. The effect is traumatic: he is bullied and finds himself torn between loyalty to his father, on one side of the green baize door that separates home from school, and loyalty to his school friends who rebel against the school's authority. Greene will come to believe that the key theme of 'divided loyalties' in his work derives from this youthful experience.

1921–29

This period begins with Graham needing psychiatric help under the supervision of Dr Kenneth Richmond in 1921 after attempting to run away from school. It ends with the successful publication of his first novel, *The Man Within* (1929), a novel which, however, deeply upsets his father, ostensibly because of its overt sexuality but perhaps also because of the antagonistic attitude of the book's hero to his own father. Like so many writers (see, for example, Arthur Miller on *All My Sons* and Tennessee Williams on *The Glass Menagerie*), Greene has vowed that, if this work were not successful, he would give up his writing ambitions: his first two novel attempts, *Anthony Sale* and *The Episode* have been rejected outright by publishers.

In 1922 he enters Balliol College, Oxford and will graduate in 1925 with a second class B.A. honours degree in History. Towards the end of his period as a student, he will briefly join the Communist Party, an association that will have repercussions later in his career when he is refused an entry visa to America, this helping to fuel an anti-Americanism in his work that is to last a lifetime. On leaving Oxford, he lands a job with the *Nottingham Journal*, an experience he will use a decade later in the thriller *A Gun for Sale* (1936) which is set in Nottingham. He moves from there to *The Times*, where he works as a subeditor between 1926 and 1930 before embarking on his ambition to be a full-time writer.

Two key events

Around the age of twenty, Greene plays Russian Roulette with himself using his elder brother's revolver. He writes about the experience in the essay 'The Revolver in the Corner Cupboard,' which will be published in the collection *The Lost Childhood* (1951) but will be omitted from the *Collected Essays* of 1969, perhaps because he will repeat the story in his autobiography *A Sort of Life* (1971). But is it true? The biographers are divided: his official biographer, Norman Sherry is convinced of its veracity, whilst Michael Shelden and Anthony Mockler are sceptical. But if it is not true, why does Greene keep reiterating it? In any event, it is a tale that will contribute powerfully to the Greene 'myth' of the suicidal melancholic who risks death to alleviate depression (which he calls 'boredom'). It becomes part of Greene's self-definition.

The second key event is his conversion to Roman Catholicism. This is prompted by his falling in love with a Catholic convert, Vivien Dayrell-Browning, an employee of Basil Blackwell, who has published his volume of verse *Babbling April* (1925). He and Vivien will marry in 1927 and will subsequently have two children, a daughter, Lucy Caroline and a son, Francis. To learn more about Vivien's religion, Greene drops a note into Nottingham Cathedral in 1925 asking for instruction in Catholicism; on 28 February 1926, he is 'conditionally baptised'. Although he will always insist that he is not a Catholic novelist but a novelist who happens to be a Catholic, the religious dimension of his work will prove profoundly significant. It will infuse works as diverse as the gangster thriller, *Brighton Rock* (1938) and the philosophical picaresque comedy, *Monsignor Quixote* (1982); and it will be at the core of what many regard as his greatest novel, *The Power and the Glory* (1940).

1930–40

He begins the decade with two novels, *The Name of Action* (1930) and *Rumour at Nightfall* (1931) that are so unsuccessful and, in his own eyes, so irredeemably bad that he will later suppress them from editions of his Collected Works. He will end the decade with two novels, *Brighton Rock* and *The Power and the Glory* whose publication alone would guarantee him a place amongst the most important novelists of the twentieth century.

The thirties prove a period of great productivity, where he averages almost a novel a year. However, with the exception of *Stamboul Train* (1932), commercial success is elusive and it is not until *Brighton Rock* that he is able to repay the advances he has received from his publisher Heinemann. Towards the end of the decade, he will begin a liaison with Dorothy Glover: she will later work alongside Greene as a fire warden during the Blitz, and, under her professional name of Dorothy Craigie, illustrate Greene's books for children.

Two key events

It is at this time that Greene's propensity for foreign travel particularly begins to manifest itself. His wanderlust will earn him the nickname of 'Otis B. Driftwood' (after the Groucho Marx character in *A Night at the Opera)* from Vivien. Among other places, he visits Norway and Sweden in 1933; Paris in 1934; Liberia in 1935, with his cousin Barbara (who will write about the experience in her book, *Land Benighted* in 1938); and Mexico and France in 1938. His visits to Liberia and Mexico will provide the substance of his travel books, *Journey Without Maps* (1936) and *The Lawless Roads* (1939), respectively: whilst Sweden and Mexico will be deployed as expressive backgrounds in his novels *England Made Me* and *The Power and the Glory*. No English novelist will subsequently make more extensive or eloquent use of foreign settings.

The second key element is Greene's growing involvement with the cinema. He becomes film critic of *The Spectator* from 1935 to 1940 and also of the periodical *Night and Day*, where a notorious review of the Shirley Temple movie, *Wee Willie Winkie* (1937) prompts litigation proceedings from its outraged makers, Twentieth Century Fox. He begins writing screenplays, notably for *Twenty-One Days* (1937), an adaptation of Galsworthy which Greene, the critic, candidly tears to shreds on its release; but his keen eye for film style and kinetics begins to feed imaginatively and beneficially into his fiction, and his association with the cinema will reap great rewards.

1941–51

In 1941, Greene is recruited into the Secret Intelligence Service (SIS) (MI6) at the instigation of his younger sister Elisabeth who works for the Service and who is to marry one of its most important employees, Rodney Dennys. Between 1941 and 1944, Greene runs a spy agency in Freetown, Sierra Leone and is known as Officer 59200, something to which he will later allude in his lampoon of British Intelligence in *Our Man in Havana* (1958). He will become friendly at this time with Kim Philby, later exposed as a double agent who will defect to the Soviet Union.

After leaving the SIS, Greene becomes a director of the publishing firm, Eyre & Spottiswoode (1944–48). His first post-war novel, *The Heart of the Matter* (1948) is a huge success.

Key events

At the end of 1946, Greene begins an intense affair with Catherine Walston, wife of a wealthy landowner Henry Walston who will become a labour peer. Greene will propose marriage and the relationship will provide the basis for his novel, *The End of the Affair* (1951).

Greene's mastery of the film medium will reach its zenith between 1947 and 1949. He will script a fine film version of his novel, *Brighton Rock* (1947) and have his happiest and most fruitful collaboration with the director Carol Reed on *The Fallen Idol* (1948) and the immortal *The Third Man* (1949).

1952–60

A period which sees a shift of interest in his work from religion to politics. He is the Indo-China correspondent for *The New Republic* in 1954. His novel, *The Quiet American* (1955) is prophetic about future conflict in Vietnam, just as his satire *Our Man In Havana* seems, in some of its details, to anticipate the Cuban missile crisis of the early 1960s.

The decade sees more travel, publishing responsibilities and amours. Among other places, he visits Malaya and French Indo-China (1952); Vietnam (1953); Kenya (1954); Vietnam and Haiti (1956); China and Cuba (1957); and the Congo (1959). He will become a director of the Bodley Head publishing company (1958–64): one of his coups will be to persuade Charlie Chaplin to write his autobiography. He becomes romantically involved with the Australian painter and theatre designer Jocelyn Rickards and later with the Swedish actress Anita Bjork.

Key events

Greene has a change from the solitude of novel-writing when he moves to the communal activity of writing for the stage. He has two striking West End successes, *The Living Room* (1953), which becomes a personal triumph for the young actress Dorothy Tutin, and *The Complaisant Lover* (1959), starring Ralph Richardson and directed by John Gielgud.

Greene's frequent bouts of depression are at their worst during this period. Friends feel his obsessive visiting of international trouble spots is his oblique way of sidestepping the Catholic sin of suicide by placing himself in dangerous situations that increase his likelihood of getting killed: some feel he is unlikely to survive the decade.

This phase will culminate in the publication of his most anguished, cathartic novel, *A Burnt-Out Case* (1961).

1961–69

The decade begins with arguably his gloomiest work, *A Burnt-Out Case*; it ends with his most cheerful, *Travels With My Aunt* (1969).

He meets Yvonne Cloetta who will remain a devoted companion for the last thirty years of his life. She will be instrumental in his decision to settle in Antibes from 1966, along with, he says, 'good wine and good bread'.

He travels widely during the 1960s, his locations including Moscow, East Germany, Jamaica, Haiti, Cuba, Israel, Paraguay and Czechoslovakia. He meets Fidel Castro in 1964. A lighter tone comes into his work in the collection of short stories, *May We Borrow Your Husband?* (1967). Ironically, however, a novel called *The Comedians* (1966) is one of his grimmest novels, an indictment of the brutal regime in Haiti of Papa Doc, which prompts a response from the dictator's 'Department of Foreign Affairs' in the form of a pamphlet entitled *Graham Greene Unmasked* where the novelist is accused of being (for starters) a sadist, a spy, a torturer and a drug addict. Greene is flattered: it demonstrates that his novel has 'drawn blood'.

Two key combative statements from the period – on commitment and loyalty – will reverberate and be reviewed for years after by Greene followers: Dr Magiot in the final chapter of *The Comedians*: 'Catholics and Communists have committed great crimes, but at least they have not stood aside, like an established society, and been indifferent. I would rather have blood on my hands than water like Pilate.'

Greene, accepting the Shakespeare prize at the University of Hamburg in 1969 and offering as the theme of his lecture, 'The Virtue of Disloyalty': 'Isn't it the story-teller's task to act as the devil's advocate...? The writer is driven by his own vocation to...see the virtues of the Capitalist in a Communist society, of the Communist in a Capitalist state...He stands for the victims, and the victims change.'

In effect, he is only reiterating what he said about the writer's role twenty years before in *Why Do I Write?* (1948). But it resonates defiantly, coming only a year after the furore provoked by his defence of his friend and Soviet spy, Kim Philby in his introduction to Philby's book, *My Silent War* (1968).

1970–80

The decade is framed by the publication of two volumes of autobiography, *A Sort of Life* in 1971 and *Ways of Escape* in 1980. He becomes ever more involved in the politics of South and Central America. He meets Allende in Chile in 1971, two years before the CIA inspired military coup; he befriends General Torrijos of Panama (1976) and will later commemorate him in *Getting to know the General* (1984); and he is a member of the Panamanian delegation to Washington for the signing of the Canal Treaty (1977). Dorothy Glover dies in 1971; Catherine Walston in 1978.

Key event

The publication of the two great novels of his last period, *The Honorary Consul* (1973) and *The Human Factor* (1978).

1981–91

At a lecture at the National Film Theatre in London in 1983, Greene is asked why his books are getting shorter and shorter. 'Because I'm getting older and older,' he replies.

Productivity is inevitably winding down, but flashes of the old magic are still evident in the benign humour of *Monsignor Quixote* (1982) and the mischievous plot twists of *The Captain and the Enemy* (1988). The combative spirit resurfaces in *J'Accuse* (1982), an exposé of organised crime in Nice and written in defence of Yvonne Cloetta's daughter, Martine. As the end nears, prizes accumulate and old haunts are revisited. In Russia in 1986, he receives a large sum of money owed in back royalties for his books, and he donates most of it to the Foundation helping the children of Chernobyl. He also looks up Philby, who expresses the view on Moscow television that *The Quiet American* is the book of Greene's that is closest to perfection: 'It is a perfect criticism of the CIA...I am not going to state that he doesn't like Americans, but...the American chauvinism, their principle that they can teach people how to live – this Graham hates.' The mark of a great writer: the diversity of opinion over what constitutes his greatest work.

Key event

Greene dies of a blood disease in Vevey, Switzerland (the land of the cuckoo clock) on 3 April 1991.

Awards and Honours

Hawthornden Prize, 1940, for *The Power and the Glory*; the James Tait Black Memorial Prize, 1949, for *The Heart of the Matter*; the Catholic Literary Award, 1952, for *The End of the Affair*; Boys' Club of America Junior Book Award, 1955, for *The Little Horse Bus*; Pietzak Award, Poland, 1960; D.Litt., Cambridge University, 1962; Balliol College, Oxford, honorary fellow, 1963; Companion of Honour, 1966; D.Litt., University of Edinburgh, 1967; Shakespeare Prize, University of Hamburg, 1969; Legion d'Honneur, chevalier, 1969; John Dos Passos Prize, 1980; Medal of the city of Madrid, 1980; Jerusalem Prize, 1981; Grand Cross of the Order of Vasco Nunez de Balboa (Panama), 1983; named commander of the Order of Arts and Letters (France), 1984; named to British Order of Merit, 1986; named to the Order of Ruben Dario (Nicaragua), 1987; Royal Society of Literature Prize, 1989.

Introduction: Secret Sharer

Nobody who lives escapes a private agony.

– Graham Greene[1]

In itself, the practice of deception is not particularly exacting; it is a matter of experience, of professional expertise, it is a facility most of us can acquire. But while a confidence trickster, a play-actor or a gambler can return from his performance to the ranks of his admirers, the secret agent enjoys no such relief. For him, deception is first a matter of self-defence. He must protect himself not only from without but from within, against the most natural of impulses; though he earn a fortune, his role may forbid him the purchase of a razor, though he be erudite, it can befall him to mumble nothing but banalities; though he be an affectionate husband and father, he must under all circumstances withhold himself from those in whom he should naturally confide.

– John Le Carré[2]

I think she was a Catholic – of a people that can think thoughts alien to ours and keep them to themselves.

– Ford Madox Ford[3]

When in Moscow in 1987, Graham Greene was asked by a television interviewer what made him write. 'I don't know,' he replied. 'It's like an illness. It's like a boil on one's cheek and at a certain moment you feel you have to scratch it off. Life would be impossible for me if I knew that I would never write another book.' It is said of the great

9

composer prodigy, Erich Wolfgang Korngold that, as a child, he was so voracious for knowledge and accomplishment that his parents would reward him for *not* playing the piano or reading a book by Nietzsche. Greene had something of the same artistic temperament and compulsion. Some writers need to take tablets to stimulate them into writing; Greene had to take pills in order to stop himself from writing. He would have echoed the sentiment of his favourite Russian writer, Anton Chekhov, who stated in a letter of 27 March 1894: 'Not for a minute am I free of the thought that I must, am obliged to write. Write, write and write.'[4]

This is a biography of Greene, the writer – a literary biography. That is to say, it does not attempt to duplicate the comprehensiveness of Norman Sherry's heroic investigation and account of Greene's life, where the phrase 'following in his master's footsteps' has been taken to an almost literal extreme. Nor does it aim for the contentiousness of Sherry's rival biographer, Michael Shelden, who seems disillusioned by his subject before he has reached page twenty. Although much of this text has been written in the same spirit in which that great conductor, Klaus Tennstedt instructed the London Philharmonic Orchestra to tackle the last movement of Mahler's titanic Sixth Symphony ('Play it as if you hate it'), the pain and anger has mainly come from external circumstances: my admiration for Greene as man and writer has remained undiminished. There are other biographies which have concentrated on different aspects of Greene's extraordinarily varied life – for example, that of Bill West, who has particularly uncovered material relating to Greene's work with British Intelligence; or of Father Leopoldo Duran, following and describing Greene's religious development and doubts during the final part of his life; or of William Cash, giving a rather lurid view of Greene's love life and particularly his affair with Catherine Walston; or of Anthony Mockler, the most anguished of all as he tries to bring together the public, private and secret strands of Greene's life. Greene was a many-faceted writer whose different skills had a wide-ranging appeal amongst his peers and successors, so that John Le Carré could exhibit particular interest in his spy novels, V.S. Pritchett particular admiration for his literary criticism, and Paul Theroux enormous respect for his travel writing which, he thought, anticipated much of modern journalism in its evocative descriptions of individual stories in war-torn countries. To each his own Greene. My concentration is on a biographical narrative that traces the trajectory and characteristics of the literary career: the kind of writer he became, and why.

The book, therefore, explores a few basic questions to do with Greene's literary life. We know he had a compulsion to write, but what was the initial motivation for becoming a writer? We know that Greene was enormously well read, had a vast collection of books, held influential positions in major publishing houses: indeed, aside from collecting car numbers, his only hobby seems to have been touring second-hand bookshops. He acknowledged that books had a big influence on him: which are the works that had this effect, and how was his own work changed as a result? As a professional writer, Greene was prolific and enormously disciplined: what were the routines he regularly followed to keep up his productivity?

There are some unusual features connected with Greene's literary career that have also been investigated. He was fond of – indeed, obsessive about – augmenting his fictional texts with epigraphs and dedications that contain fascinating clues both on the underlying intention of the novel and on his personal life at the time: they generate a compelling sub-textual meaning of their own which warrants exploration. Greene has been seen as a serious, seedy chronicler of sex, sin and salvation[5] but a somewhat neglected aspect of his art is his sense of comedy. It is discussed here as an aspect of his literary development that had its source in a crucial turning point in his personal life, which both rejuvenated his writing and may even have saved him from suicide.

A particular feature of this text is the emphasis given to the importance of the cinema in Greene's work, something he always acknowledged but which, understandably, because of the literary provenance of the critic, has rarely been granted proper attention. (It was a tone Greene himself did not adopt: he was passionate, not patronising, about films.) In his book on Greene, Atkins (1957) wrote that 'the filmic quality of Greene's fiction has frequently been pointed out and as often praised. In fact, it is his worst work which invites the film comparison'.[6] I could not disagree more with this comment, and the intensity of my disagreement has been the motivation and spur towards giving this aspect of Greene's writing career special attention. There have, of course, been fine studies of the relationship between Greene and the cinema before, notably Judith Adamson's perceptive work, Quentin Falk's stimulating survey of cinematic adaptations of Greene, and David Parkinson's invaluable anthology of Greene's writings on the cinema. But I have attempted to widen the discussion beyond the issues of adaptation of Greene or the values of his film criticism to embrace a consideration of how the cinema helped shape his literary style at a crucial point in his writing career and how some films seem to have had an enormous impact on his critical and literary sensibility. In this latter respect, I have drawn particular attention to his reviews of William Wyler's *These Three* (1936), whose dramatisation of childhood evil and the psychological sadism of the school bully struck a particular chord with him; and Julien Duvivier's *Pépé le Moko* (1936), whose skill at evoking what Greene called the 'experience of exile' and the 'absurd, passionate tangle of emotions which make up the mind'[7] seems to anticipate the aspirations of his own fiction. As an indulgence, in the manner of *Travels With My Aunt* (and encouraged by an observation of Neil Jordan's in his Foreword to *Travels in Greeneland* – see Chapter 8), an extended comparison of Greene and Alfred Hitchcock has also been included to reveal coincidental connections and cross-references that intriguingly bind together two of the greatest popular artists in their respective fields of the twentieth century.

In the radio programme 'Greene at 80,' broadcast by the BBC in 1984, Father Leopoldo Duran is heard to say at one stage: 'I am very doubtful if it is possible to write a real biography of Graham Greene.' (At the time of writing, Norman Sherry still has not quite got there; and, at the annual Greene Festival in Berkhamsted in October 1999, Father Duran was scathing about Michael Shelden's version of the life, calling it infamous, impudent and mendacious.) From whatever perspective he is viewed, Greene is an enormously elusive personality. Secretive by nature from childhood, for reasons described in a later chapter, he was later to practise secrecy as a profession for British Intelligence; and combining all that with the requirements of the secret agent outlined by John Le Carre in the epigraph to this chapter, it is not surprising that expertise in evasion or limited disclosure became almost second nature to him. Even his handwriting implies a secretive nature: it is barely decipherable. In a BBC Radio programme about Greene's life and work, broadcast in October 1979, Paul Theroux said of him: 'He had perfected an attitude and way of presenting himself in which he could disclose nothing he didn't want to disclose.' (That is another characteristic he shared with that master of cautious self-projection, Alfred Hitchcock, who, in interviews, never lowered his guard.) Until late in his life, he refused to be interviewed on television because he thought you became an actor when you were being filmed and, in any case, thought it might restrict his movements and his capacity to observe if he were widely recognised: it is worth remembering that even as dedicated a bibliophile as Francois Truffaut failed to recognise him when he cast him in a role for his film, *Day for Night* (1973). Indeed, the term 'literary biography' has, I believe, a peculiar applicability to Greene. He mixed literature with biography, fiction with fact, which, as Tyler tells Holly Martins after his forlorn British Council lecture in *The Third Man*, is a 'pretty dangerous' mixture, like 'oil and water'. In fact, if there be one truth above all others about Greene, I would say it is this: that his autobiographies are less self-revealing than they might appear and that his fiction is more autobiographical than he would have us believe.

In a section on Shakespeare in his 1942 study, *British Dramatists* (the first epigraph of this chapter), Greene makes reference to what he calls 'the private agony' which he seems to think is an inescapable fact of human existence. In his case, this 'private agony' manifested itself in what he was to call 'boredom' but which Norman Sherry thought was his euphemism for profound depression. The roots of that depression lay in his childhood – 'he hated most of his youth', opined Tynan (1989) in his *Harper's Bazaar* profile of Greene[8] – and was later in his life played off against his Catholicism, which served as a moral authority against which he could react and as a set of doctrinal ideals against which he could, like Scobie in *The Heart of the Matter*, masochistically measure his failure as a human being. The infamous 'Russian roulette' episode of his youth is all part of this, as is his precocious submission to psychoanalysis in his teens under the supervision of Dr Kenneth Richmond. But in his autobiography, *A Sort of Life*, Greene rejects psychoanalysis as any permanent answer to his problems. He quotes Rilke: 'Psychoanalysis is too fundamental a help for me, it helps you once and for all, it clears you up, and to find myself cleared up one day might be even more helpless than this chaos.'[9] In effect, Greene's writing became his psychoanalysis, his catharsis and his purgation. It was his essential means of sharing his secrets and grappling with the demons within, as he mapped out a moral, emotional and narrative terrain – sometimes referred to as 'Greeneland'[10] – that was his alone and which brought out all his gifts as a novelist. 'You don't know him from his face, or the way he speaks,' concluded Paul Theroux in the 1979 BBC interview mentioned earlier. 'But from his writing, you know everything.'

1
Why Do I Write?

> Isn't our attitude to all our characters more or less – There, and
> may God forgive me, goes myself?
>
> – Graham Greene[1]

In the preface to his classic satirical novel, *Joseph Andrews* (1742),
Henry Fielding refers ironically to the then Poet Laureate, Colley
Cibber, who had recently published his autobiography and who,
Fielding wrote, 'lived the life he recorded and is by many thought
to have lived such a life only in order to write it'.[2] Greene sometimes felt that there was too much of a critical tendency to see his
career in the same way: that is, that he lived the life he did – amorously,
adventurously – to provide the material substance of his novels. To
which he would always retort: if only writing were that easy.
Certainly he would visit the places that he knew were to provide
the settings of his novels, but that was simply for the sake of
accuracy of physical detail and perhaps as compensation for what
he called his short memory and his lack of visual imagination. So,
when researching the Swedish setting of *England Made Me*, he took
a camera as if he were scouting a location; and, to describe the
Assistant Commissioner's journey from Piccadilly in *It's A Battlefield*
(1934), he paced out the journey himself street by street. But this is
background filling, not creative inspiration. As Hawtree (1989)
has pointed out, there is a world of difference between Greene's
reporting of an incident as a war correspondent in Vietnam and his
writing of that same incident as a dramatic narrative event in *The
Quiet American*.[3] 'All that we can easily recognise as our experience

in a novel is mere reporting: it has a place but an unimportant one...', Greene wrote. 'Perhaps a novelist has a greater ability to forget than other men – he has to forget or become sterile. *What he forgets is the compost of the imagination.*' [my italics][4]

That last phrase seems to me a key dimension of Greene's art. As he says, creativity comes into play not from the remembrance of actuality but from the forgetting of it and the consequent fertilising of the imagination. Like much else in his work, he probably picked this up from Henry James, particularly from James's preface to his novel, *The Spoils of Poynton* (1897) when he describes the genesis of idea. Dining with friends on one Christmas eve, James happened to overhear a conversation about an old lady 'at daggers drawn with her only son over the ownership of the valuable furniture of a fine old house'. That was it: he had his situation. The key aspect of the anecdote for the novelist was that, once having heard the germ of the idea that would, as it were, furnish the novel, he did not wish to hear any more. He did not want to know how, as he put it, 'clumsy life' resolved the conflict: he wanted to 'transplant' the idea into 'richer soil' that is, fiction, art.[5] Life can suggest things but both James and Greene knew that it took an artist to turn it into enduring literature; and a simplified biographical approach to the artistic process undermines the very thing that distinguishes literature from life. Greene alluded to this in an interesting foreword he wrote to a book on hotel-keeping, *Pavilions by the Sea*, written by his friend Tom Laughton (brother of the great actor Charles Laughton). 'Rashly I encouraged him to write a book,' Greene wrote, adding, 'rashly, because the hackneyed phrase "everyone has one book inside him" is deceptive and totally untrue. Everyone has the material in his memories for many books, but that is not the same thing at all'.[6] Tellingly, he went on to quote from that passage in T.S. Eliot's *The Hollow Men* about the gap between the will and the deed, between aspiration and achievement: 'Between the idea / And the reality / Between the motion / And the act / Falls the shadow.' In the event, Greene thought Laughton had written an entertaining book, but the point remained for him that the fact that everyone has a story to tell is no guarantee of literary merit or readability.

With this in mind, I am concerned in this literary biography to keep a balance between biography and literature, an awareness of where one stops and where the other begins. One cannot eliminate the life entirely, of course, nor would one want to: the work comes from *The Man Within*. But it is a matter of emphasis: by its nature, a literary biography is as much concerned with the writer's approach to the craft of writing as with the biographical inspiration. Above all else, Greene was a supreme craftsman and immensely professional in his approach to his work, in terms of his earning potential and his disciplined approach to the physical as well as the inspirational act of writing. There is a story that Lillian Hellman would tell about herself when she was conversing with the great American critic, Edmund Wilson, who asked her what she was working on at the moment. When she told him she was not progressing with anything and had writers' block, Wilson apparently retorted: 'Foolishness. A writer writes. That's all there is to it.'[7] Greene felt that: if you call yourself a writer by trade, then you write – and not necessarily to express yourself but maybe to escape from yourself. Greene would surely have concurred with something said to an interviewer by Orson Welles: 'My work is what enables me to come out of myself. I like what I do, not what I am...Do you know the best service anyone could render to art? Destroy all biographies. Only art can explain the life of a man and not the contrary.'[8]

So why did Greene become a writer? And how might the life explain, or partially explain, what kind of writer he became? In 1948, Greene had taken part in a published exchange of views with Elizabeth Bowen and V.S. Pritchett, dedicated to the very question of why writers write. Some of Greene's comments are revealing disclosures of his views on the relationship between the writer and society, and between literature and morality. For example, he writes:

> I would like to imagine there are none but I fear there are at least two duties the novelist owes – to tell the truth as he sees it and to accept no special privileges from the state...By truth, I mean accuracy – it is largely a matter of style. One privilege he can claim, in common perhaps with his fellow human beings, but possibly with greater safety, is that of disloyalty.[9]

A little later he goes on:

> Literature has nothing to do with edification. I am not arguing literature is amoral, but that it presents a personal moral, and the personal morality of an individual is seldom identical with the

morality of the group to which he belongs. You remember the black and white squares of Bishop Blougram's chessboard. As a novelist, I must be allowed to write from the point of view of the black square as well as of the white.[10]

Yet curiously, while discussing these issues of literary concern, he does not address the title of the pamphlet: that is, he does not disclose his basic literary motivation, the reason or impulse that started him on the road as writer. It is only in the later autobiographical fragments that this question will be addressed and even here, the very titles of these disclosures – *A Sort of Life*, *Fragments of Autobiography*, *Ways of Escape* – have intimations of evasion, as if he is warning that we must not expect the whole story or the whole truth. (One is reminded of Max Beerbohm's response when asked if Frank Harris ever told the truth: 'Oh yes – when his invention flagged, you know.') Yet some sense of the inner motivation does come through.

One inescapable aspect of Greene's background as a writer is the fact that he came from an intensely literary family with a penchant for recording their experiences in books. If your first cousin twice removed on your mother's side is Robert Louis Stevenson and a contemporary cousin is Christopher Isherwood, then it is not entirely surprising that you would be drawn into carrying on the writing tradition: the instinct to publish seemed deeply rooted in the Greene families. It reminds me of that great moment in the Charlie Chaplin film, *Limelight* (1952) – and, of course, Chaplin and Greene were good friends – when Chaplin's aged clown character, Calvero is planning a theatrical comeback and tells his beloved ballerina friend (Claire Bloom) that: 'It's where I belong.' 'But I thought you hated the theatre,' she says to him, to which he responds: 'I do. I also hate the sight of blood – but it's in my veins.' That is what I have always thought about Graham Greene: that writing was in his veins.

But what was the initial impulse to write? Like so much else in Greene, the core of the motivation lay in childhood. The theme of childhood will crop up again and again in his work – from 'The Basement Room' to *Brighton Rock*, from *England Made Me* to *The Third Man* – but it is childhood not as theme but as stimulus for the literary impulse and ambition that concerns me here. Greene gives little away about this in *Why Do I Write?*, but I am tempted to draw an analogy at this point between Greene and George Orwell, who, a year earlier, had written a very personal essay on the same subject entitled *Why I Write* (1947). At one stage, Orwell states:

> I had a lonely child's habit of making up stories and holding conversations with imaginary persons, and I think from the start my literary ambitions were mixed up with the feelings of being isolated and undervalued. I knew I had a facility with words and a power of facing unpleasant facts. I felt this created a sort of private world in which I could get my own back for my failure in everyday life.[11]

Although one would not press the comparison too far, some of this is surely applicable to Greene. The idea of writing as a way of, in Orwell's phrase, 'getting your own back' is something that would have struck a chord. He approved of Gauguin's sentiment, 'Life being what it is, one dreams of revenge';[12] and the writer-hero of *The End of the Affair* reflects on revenge as a primary motive for recording his account of events in the novel (though he rejects it as the driving force). As with D.H. Lawrence, fiction in Greene sometimes seems to become a means of paying off old scores – or what the psychiatrist Edmund Bergler, in his classic study, *The Writer and Psychoanalysis*, called 'injustice collecting'. Bergler's definition of a writer was 'a person who tries to solve an inner conflict through the sublimatory medium of writing';[13] this seems to me a profoundly suggestive formulation in relation to Greene's work.

Even more intriguing in Orwell's account of his writing motivation was his intuition of its connection with his childhood feeling of being, as he put it, 'isolated and *undervalued*' [my italics]. In the cases of both Orwell and Greene, this was particularly intensified by their experience at public school. Much has been written and speculated about the significance of Greene's school experience in the formation of his character and his artistry – by Greene himself, it should be said, as well as by his commentators – and particularly the significance of his being bullied at school by two pupils whom he called Carter (the principal tormentor) and Watson. References and allusions to that experience are scattered all over his work, in publications as diverse as the droll comedy thriller *Our Man in Havana*, where Wormold's intended assassin is called Carter, and his introduction to Marjorie Bowen's 1906 novel, *The Viper of Milan*, where he says: 'as for Visconti, with his beauty, his patience, and his genius for evil, I had watched him pass by many a time in his black Sunday suit smelling of mothballs. His name was Carter. He exercised terror from a distance like a snow-cloud over the young fields'.[14] There is some disagreement amongst scholars over whether Greene embellished or exaggerated this memory of psychological distress. How true it is seems to me of no more ultimate importance, comparatively speaking, than whether, say, the twelve-year-old Dickens really was treated as badly in the blacking factory as he said or whether the five-year-old Alfred Hitchcock was actually locked up in a police cell as a practical joke by a policeman friend of his father. What is more significant is the way these artists consciously (even, self-consciously) built those events into a personal mythology of creative motivation, as a key to their artistic ambitions, predilections and personalities. The same kind of thing is at work in Greene.

In *A Sort of Life*, Greene gives an account of meeting Watson again in 1951 in Kuala Lumpur when they are both middle aged, and being quite disarmed by Watson's nostalgic memory of their schooldays and of how inseparable the three of them had been. For years Greene had dreamt of a reunion like this and of getting revenge by humiliating Carter or Watson in public, only to find that, when he does bump into Watson, the meeting is a complete anticlimax. (Carter is now dead, Greene is told.[15]) What is tremendously suggestive, though, is Greene's reflection on this encounter:

> I wondered all the way back to the hotel if I would ever have written a book had it not been for Watson and the dead Carter, if those years of humiliation had not given me an *excessive* [my italics] desire to prove I was good at something, however long the effort might prove.[16]

Greene always used adjectives with the utmost fastidiousness in his writing so I am struck by his use of the word 'excessive' in that passage – as if signalling an awareness of an overreaction to this childhood trauma, almost as if it provided an excuse rather than a reason for writing, that the account of this trauma served a particular need. My inclination is still to take the passage as one of the most sincere and revealing that Greene ever wrote. It connects with something he had written a few pages earlier in the same chapter: 'I was very bad at gymnastics [at school] and all life long my instinct has been to abandon anything for which I have no talent. Tennis, golf, dancing, sailing have all been abandoned, and perhaps it is only desperation that keeps me writing, like someone who clings to an unhappy marriage for fear of solitude.'[17] It was not desperation that kept Greene writing, surely: it was self-esteem. Writing throughout his life was intimately bound up with a sense of self-value, self-worth and love of self. To borrow his own phrase, it was the thing above all that demonstrated that 'he was good at something', which he had felt an 'excessive' desire to prove. That desire was rooted to that childhood experience, and childhood is the capital on which every writer can draw.

In *Ways of Escape*, he suggested another major motivation behind his writing: namely, writing as therapy, a means of escape from what he called 'the madness, the melancholia, the panic-fear which is inherent in the human situation'.[18] It was an escape from boredom, he would argue, which can be linked with his obsessive need to set his novels in contemporary flashpoints where danger seems guaranteed. Escape was vital because ennui could lead to a mood of suicidal depression that, he feared, he may have inherited from his maternal grandfather who had ended his life in an asylum.[19] The manic-depressive, he felt, was always walking on thin ice and should therefore not stay long in the same place for fear the ice will break, which can be offered as another reason for his obsessive travelling and restlessness.

As a coda, though, one should say that none of this therapeutic need would have been of much literary consequence if it had not been attached to two attributes vital to any major writer: a sense of observation and a sense of curiosity. Again it is Henry James who put it best when he spelt out the single piece of advice he would offer to any aspiring novelist: 'Try to be one of the people on whom nothing is lost!'[20] That seems to me a major part of Greene's genius: the sense he gave of someone who observed and absorbed everything, which would later come out in a form perhaps very different from the way in which it was first perceived. No reader could forget the account he gives in *A Sort of Life* of the unexpected death in hospital of a ten-year-old child. Greene was in an adjoining bed recovering from an appendix operation when it happened (the year was 1931) and, while feeling the human tragedy unfold around him, he could not suppress the writer within him keenly observing the grief-stricken reaction of relatives – the inability of language to convey the depth of their feelings. He quotes Flaubert here about the inadequacy of language to convey the inexpressible: 'Human language is like a cracked kettle on which we beat out tunes for bears to dance to, when all the time we are longing to move the stars to pity.' Nor could he resist the novelistic instinct to digest this for possible future use in his work. 'There is a splinter of ice in the heart of every writer,' he concluded.[21] In my view, he was later to make use of this observation, but to transform in a compassionate way. In the film *The Third Man*, there is a crucial scene that will finally and irrevocably turn Holly (Joseph Cotten) against his lifelong friend Harry Lime (Orson Welles) and persuade him to betray Lime to the authorities, and it takes place in a children's hospital. Holly has been lured into visiting the hospital by Major Calloway (Trevor Howard) and sees for himself the appalling effect that the dilution of penicillin (the racket Harry is in) has had on these children. Because of the discretion of Carol Reed's direction, we are not shown anything but Holly's reaction and a final shot of a discarded teddy bear that implies the death of its former owner.[22] But the implication is clear. 'You win, Calloway,' he says, capitulating to Calloway's quite calculated, almost cynical strategy to bring about Holly's change of heart that will enable him to catch the fugitive. There is a splinter of ice in Calloway too: not surprising perhaps that, in a notably well acted film, Trevor Howard's performance was Greene's favourite of the lot.

2
The Books in My Life

The influence of early books is profound. So much of the future lies on the shelves: early reading has more influence on conduct than any religious teaching.

– Graham Greene[1]

On one point, and perhaps only one point, do Graham Greene's accounts of his own life carry the ring of truth, and that is when they deal with the books and the authors that influenced him. It is as though this, and this alone, is too important not to be entirely accurate. All the rest may when necessary be twisted and turned, dramatized, edited out, cut, exaggerated, run together or, as the case may be, respected in order to make a better or at least a more coherent story. But books – the centre, after all, of any writer's life – are sacred.

– Anthony Mockler[2]

Said the great conductor Herbert Von Karajan about his arch-rival Leonard Bernstein (and it was a compliment he paid to few fellow musicians): 'He's full of music.' The same kind of compliment could be paid to Greene: he's full of literature. When reading a book of his, one feels as if one is reading several books, so packed are they with allusions, parallels and evocations: they breathe the air of a cultured man steeped in the literature of his and earlier times. It is one of the reasons for the deceptive richness of his novels, the revelation of a depth that goes beyond fascinations of plot and character in the thriller mode. Entertaining and individualistic, Greene also carries with him the resonance of an older and distinguished literary tradition. He not only absorbed what he observed for future use in his novels but also absorbed what he read. As important to his literary biography as the life in his books were the books in his life.

Take *The Human Factor*, for example: the novel is crammed with suggestive bookish allusions. It takes its epigraph from Joseph Conrad ('I only know that he who forms a tie is lost. The germ of corruption has entered his soul') to preface a tale of fidelity and betrayal that Conrad said were the driving themes of his own work. A reference to Rider Haggard's Allan Quatermain in Part 3 Chapter 3 is both a reminiscence of a childhood favourite of Greene's and, more significantly in the context of the novel, a revelation of Castle's idealisation of himself as an adventurer in Africa. Amongst other references, there are allusions to Trollope, whom Hargreaves reads as an analogue to his mood and a novel of whose is Castle's last present from his contact, Mr Halliday; and in the final part of the novel, when stranded in Moscow, Castle takes to reading *Robinson Crusoe*, recognising that, like Crusoe, he too has no soul to speak to or confide in. (Greene might also have been alluding to the fact that Daniel Defoe also made a living from being a spy.) To enrich the density of his work, literary analogy seems almost a reflex action in Greene: it came to him as naturally as breathing. In her reminiscence, *Greene on Capri: A Memoir* (London: Virago Press, 2000), Shirley Hazzard noted that they first became acquainted through her overhearing a conversation between Greene and his companion at a table in Capri and her being able to complete a quotation from Browning that Greene had started, which, in Greene's terms, was clearly a good augury for friendship. A volume has even been assembled on the contents of Greene's own library and his annotations of the books for clues they might yield (not always reliable, I would think) about his works and personality.[3]

'Literature was the longest and most consistent pleasure of Graham's life,' wrote Shirley Hazzard.[4] As well as being full of literary references, his novels have their literariness built sometimes into their narrative structure, as can be seen with the hero of *The Confidential Agent* (1939), who is a literary scholar, and the Secret Service codebook used by Wormold in *Our Man in Havana*, which is Lamb's *Tales from Shakespeare*. Apart from his own creative output, he wrote appreciative critical essays on a wide range of authors such as James, Dickens, Fielding and Sterne, Mauriac, Ford Maddox Ford, Buchan,

Beatrix Potter, Samuel Butler, George Moore, Somerset Maughan, Edgar Wallace, Rider Haggard and Hans Christian Andersen (whom he refers to as 'that wise author' in his introduction to *The Human Factor*). He wrote introductions to the works of novelists such as Patricia Highsmith and R.K. Narayan; and the latter, along with, for example, Muriel Spark, was an author for whom Greene's admiration also extended to material assistance. He worked as managing director of the publishing firm, Eyre & Spottiswoode between 1944 and 1948, and later for the Bodley Head.[5] He absorbed the influence of writers he esteemed and from whom he felt he could learn, but not in the sense of conscious borrowing. 'Immature poets imitate; mature poets steal,' wrote T.S. Eliot in his essay on Philip Massinger in *The Sacred Wood* (1920). Greene stole: and it is a measure of his artistry that, with a literary background which might have overwhelmed or blocked another writer's imagination, he could still create a world – Greeneland, if you will – that was distinctively his and no one else's. At the same time, one cannot fully assimilate and credit what Greene wrote without taking into account what he read, its effect on him, his usage of that effect. As with his observation, so with his reading: he was someone on whom nothing was lost.

An exhaustive pursuit of the literary influences on Greene is beyond the scope of this – arguably, any – book, but there are a few of especial significance in the light they throw on his writing career and development. An obvious starting point would be Joseph Conrad. In *Ways of Escape*, Greene mentions how an early novel of his, *Rumour at Nightfall*, which he later suppressed, had been contaminated by the influence of Conrad's *Arrow of Gold*.[6] He resolved to stop reading Conrad because he felt he was having too great an imprint on his own literary style, a resolution he claimed he kept for nearly thirty years until he found himself reading *Heart of Darkness* on a journey to the Congo while researching *A Burnt-Out Case*.[7] Nevertheless, one can continue to see Greene as Conrad's successor in the way his works evoke the fascination of exotic places; explore the impact of place on character; observe the spectacle of civilised man going to seed in foreign lands; and probe obsessively the all-too-human characteristic of betrayal – of one's country, one's friends and oneself. Watts (1997) has argued persuasively that *It's A Battlefield* owes a lot to Conrad's *The Secret Agent*;[8] and Lodge (1997) has suggested that the controversy over the Catholicism in *The Heart of the Matter* might have obscured an indebtedness the novel owes to *Heart of Darkness*, indicated not only by the similarity of title but by their similarly stringent critiques of colonialism.[9] It has always seemed to me that the relationship between Holly Martins and Harry Lime in *The Third Man* owes its pattern to the Marlow/Kurtz relationship in *Heart Of Darkness*: in both cases one can see the attraction and fascination of the ostensibly 'good' character for the ostensibly 'evil' character who makes him uncomfortably aware of darker potentialities within himself that he would rather not see. In Greene's screenplay, Lime is the suppressed Dionysiac side of Martins' inhibited personality, representing an out-lawed vitality which Martins both envies and fears. Marlow has the same ambivalence towards Kurtz; and in both cases, the temptation of irresponsible licence that this 'double' represents is to be rooted out in a symbolic confrontation in darkness – in Conrad's case, in the heart of the jungle; in Greene's case, in the sewers of Vienna.

As important as Conrad to Greene was Henry James. Towards the end of his life, Greene did confess to Shirley Hazzard that he now found James's final novels – *The Wings of the Dove, The Golden Bowl* – unreadable, but that is not an uncommon experience: one thinks of Alec Guinness's account in his final journal of making another attempt at reading *The Wings of the Dove* and nearly passing out with exhaustion.[10] Nevertheless, during his tenure as a managing director at Eyre & Spottiswoode, Greene had published a new edition of *The Wings of the Dove* with an introduction by Herbert Read and for most of his life, James remained a decisive influence. James's fascination with and insights into lost innocence and European corruption undoubtedly found an echo in Greene: one can find his imaginative variations on the theme of the American 'innocent' abroad in works like *The Third Man* and *The Quiet American*, just as a tale of innocence lost like 'The Basement Room' (with its situation of a child stumbling across adult perfidy and passion, with long-term tragic consequences) owes much to the example of James's *The Turn of the Screw*, which Greene always felt had a much stronger sense of evil than *Heart of Darkness*. The novelist, Bendrix, Greene's slippery alter ego in *The End of the Affair*, cites Henry James in the opening chapter as someone who guided him in his initial research that led to his meeting Henry and Sarah. Indeed, as important to Greene as James's novelistic practice were James's meditations on that practice. These were expounded in his magnificent Prefaces, which Greene devoured with the same enthusiasm to find out about his craft as he had Percy Lubbock's classic 1921 text, *The Craft of Fiction* (which, of course, so often uses James as the shining example). The Prefaces, with their insights into the whole business of novel-writing – how you use minor characters, the selection of point of view, the indivisibility of plot and character, the technical nuts and bolts of putting a novel together and making it work – had an enormous impact on Greene. One can see this particularly in *Ways of Escape*, where Greene gives an account of the genesis of his novels and his technical assessment of what did or did not work. Two examples of this are the entirely functional use he intended for the minor character of Minty in *England Made Me*, which somehow got lost under the sheer vitality of the portraiture and unbalanced the novel; and the first-person narrative that he adopted in *The End of the Affair*, partly because he felt he had been getting a bit too predictable in formal terms – and in terms of critical response – and therefore felt almost obliged to set himself a technical challenge. In Greene's view, he only partially succeeded but he learnt from it enough to make his later deployment of the technique in *The Quiet American* much more successful.

Of his immediate contemporaries, there was no writer Greene admired more than T.S. Eliot: indeed, Greene's friend, Michael Meyer defined the feeling as amounting to a sense of awe. Eliot is the source of the epigraph for one of Greene's suppressed novels, *The Name of Action* – the same quotation from *The Hollow Men* that he also cites in his intro- duction to Tom Laughton's *Pavilions by the Sea* – and for no other reason than to suggest a significance and importance that the novel does not manage to deliver: between the aspiration and the achievement has fallen the shadow of failure. What Greene treasured about Eliot, I suspect, was both his unforgettable imagistic rendering of the seediness of modern civilisation and yet the paradoxical spiritual dimensions of his work that arise in compensation from this despair. If Eliot's *The Waste Land* is the definitive evocation of post-World War One decadence, demoralisation and dismay, the equivalent work of art of post-World War Two, I would argue, is Carol Reed's film of Greene's *The Third Man*. With its babble of languages, its heap of broken images, its extraordinary visual depiction of a devastated Vienna that looks like a whole culture in ruins, and an unforgettable villain whose amoral and egoistic cynicism seems a convincing legacy from a genocidal war, *The Third Man* quite transcends its thriller genre.

Greene has moulded instead a remarkable metaphorical statement about a post-war malaise – physical, political, spiritual and psychological – in the way Eliot fashioned *The Waste Land* with different expressive means.

In *A Sort of Life*, Greene wrote – indeed, unusually, he made the point twice at different stages of the book – that 'literature can be a far more lasting influence than religious teaching'.[11] The example he had in mind was the poetry of Robert Browning. He had been given a volume of Browning's poetry as a confirmation present by his father, but the young man found the impact of the verse more sensual than spiritual. 'With Robert Browning,' he wrote, 'I lived in a region of adulteries, of assignations at dark street corners, of lascivious priests and hasty dagger thrusts, and of sexual passion far more heady than romantic love. Did my father, under that potent spell, not even notice the meaning of the lines he read us?'[12] Some lines, Greene was to say, stayed in his mind for fifty years. In his 1951 book on Greene, Kenneth Allott mentions what he calls an unconscious reference to Browning's 'The Bishop Orders His Tomb' in *Rumour at Nightfall*. From our much fuller knowledge now of Greene's literary tastes, we can fairly assume the reference was all too conscious. Like Henry James before him (a devout Browning admirer for his ability to explore action in character more than character in action), what Greene learnt from Browning was something both thematic and technical. Browning perfected the form of dramatic monologue, where characterisation is established through the narrator's own words and through the technical and psychological sophistication of the poet's moral relativity: that is to say, the poet can allow his character to state convincingly a point of view opposed to his own, but can convincingly 'unmask' this character through an unwitting but plausible self-condemnation. The Duke in Browning's *My Last Duchess* would be the classic example of that. This species of unreliable narrator was to be deployed by Henry James with great subtlety in *The Aspern Papers* and with contentious ambiguity in *The Turn of the Screw*; and Greene undoubtedly absorbed from Browning's dramatic monologues a lot about the technique of first-person narration, notably its capacity for self-justification that could be a form of self-deception, and its potential for unconscious irony. The supreme example of this in Greene's work is *The End of the Affair*, in which Bendrix unwittingly discloses a complete misinterpretation of the motivations of human behaviour and where his first-person narration develops almost unbidden into an extended confession: for all his professing unbelief, he unburdens himself of the monologue of a Catholic convert. 'I hate You, God,' he cries, 'I hate You as though You existed;' and the capitalisation gives him away. For Bendrix's hatred, as it were, brings God's existence into being: if He did not exist, what would there be to hate? For the richness of its contradictions and paradoxes, its anguished sexual surface, its tortured religious subtext, and its sophisticated use of the monologue as an unconscious self-critique, *The End of the Affair* can be seen and prized as Greene's most Browningesque novel.

Greene came to maturity as a writer in the 1930s and, for someone of his generation and sympathies, the poet who would have been an inescapable presence was W.H. Auden. There was an undoubted empathy between them, partly because of a similarity in background (a loathed upbringing in a public school) and a similarity too in social and political views (an idiosyncratic leftism that is tested and qualified by their Catholicism in the case of the Spanish Civil War). They also shared a common interest in detective stories and even in trains, so Greene's breakthrough comes when writing *Stamboul Train* whilst listening to Arthur Honegger's *Pacific 231* to keep him in the mood, and Auden touches a popular nerve with *Night Mail*, his verse written to match the mechanistic rhythms of the London to Glasgow express and of Benjamin Britten's music in the classic 1935 GPO Film Unit documentary of that name. (Samuel Hynes was to compare *Night Mail* with Greene's *A Gun for Sale* as examples of what he called 1930s 'parable art' – works that were symbolic and moral under a realistic surface.[13]) In the November 1937 issue of *New Verse*, Greene praised Auden as the greatest living poet; and was to use an excerpt from *The Orators* as an epigraph to *Journey Without Maps*. Valentine Cunningham has noted that Greene could use the phrase 'Audenesque' in a film review for *The Spectator* of 21 February 1936 ('a really dreadful woman singer murders the Audenesque charm of "You're the Top"') with the full expectation of his readership picking up the reference.[14] Auden's pre-eminence as the literary spokesman of the decade has become something of a critical cliché, but it is interesting that by the end of the 1930s, the names of Auden and Greene were sometimes being linked. It was the American critic M.D. Zabel who, particularly in the light of *Brighton Rock*, was to label Greene as 'the Auden of the modern thriller', someone who, in memorable and accessible literary language, seems to catch and express the spirit of the times – not an age of Right and Wrong but one of Good and Evil, and where baseless optimism might be more dangerously complacent than despair.[15]

In addition to this kinship of spirit, however, what Greene and Auden shared was a particular style of dynamic, contemporary imagery. An incisive critical admirer of both writers, Richard Hoggart identified as follows some of the key characteristics of Auden's use of simile that made him perhaps the most imitated, if not the most influential, of 1930s writers: the use of the startling contrast, a mixture of the abstract and the concrete, and a habit of conveying a particular quality or idea with a strikingly modern image.[16] He then noticed some of the same features in Greene, as in one of the opening sentences of *The Ministry of Fear* (1943), when the hero is going to the fair: 'The fete called him like innocence' – a compelling instance of the combination of the concrete with the abstract. This is sometimes coupled with the use of contrast or paradox, like the comment on Scobie in *The Heart of the Matter* when Greene writes: 'Virtue, the good life, tempted him in the dark like a sin.'[17] There are also the pungently down-to-earth images. A character in the first chapter of *The Confidential Agent* is described as 'thin as celery'. In *The Heart of the Matter*, a face is described as being as 'blank as a school notice-board out of term',[18] whereas the lines on Leon's face in *The Honorary Consul* are 'like a tangle of fighting snakes'.[19] In the opening chapter of *The Quiet American*, Pyle's first appearance is described by the reporter Fowler as 'the sight of a young and unused face' being 'flung at us like a dart', which catches exactly the pinprick of surprise amongst the jaded and cynical journalists of this unexpectedly fresh and innocent visage. In an example like this, the effect, as Hoggart said of Auden, can be 'sharp and stimulating': it can also come over as desperate and bitter.[20] Still, the similarity between them is palpable. In the process of finding his own style, which included the ruthless excision of redundant or pretentious similes that he felt disfigured in *The Name of Action* and *Rumour at Nightfall*, Greene undoubtedly found Auden an invaluable guide.

Although this survey of literary influences on Greene is far from exhaustive, one big question remains: who was it that set him off on this vocation in the first place? Like so much else in Greene, the answer lay in his childhood. In his essay *The Lost Childhood*, Greene wrote:

Perhaps it is only in childhood that books have any deep influence on our lives. In later life we admire, we are entertained, we may modify some views we already hold, but we are more likely to find in books merely a confirmation of what is in our minds already...But in childhood all books are books of divination, telling us about the future, and like the fortune-teller who sees a long journey in the cards or death by water they influence the future.[21]

There is something Johnsonian about the vividness of Greene's recollections of those books that had an impact on him as a child. Just as a young Samuel Johnson was so frightened after reading the ghost-scene in *Hamlet* that he had to leave his room to reassure himself that he was back in the real world, Greene was so gripped by his childhood reading of Bram Stoker's *Dracula* that he picked his lip to the point where he drew blood. In this essay, and later in *A Sort of Life*, he recalls some of the childhood reading which might have had some bearing on his future. For example, he cites Rider Haggard's *King Solomon's Mines*, which gave him a fascination with Africa that was to be developed in his later travels – in Liberia in 1935, for example, or in Sierra Leone in 1942. As previously noted, the hero of that novel is cited in a dream of Castle's in *The Human Factor*, as he searches the interior of a dark continent for that most elusive of states – peace of mind. But if there is one literary influence from childhood more than any other to which Greene draws attention, it is to Marjorie Bowen's novel, *The Viper of Milan*, published in 1906 and which Greene read at the age of fourteen (astonishingly, Marjorie Bowen was not much older than that when she wrote it). From that moment, he wrote, 'the future for better or worse really struck. From that moment I began to write. All the other possible futures slid away: the potential civil servant, the don, the clerk had to look for other incarnations.'[22]

It is curious that most critical commentators on Greene have made so little of his enthusiasm for Bowen's novel, other than to note an allusion to the text in *Travels With My Aunt* (the villains of both novels are called Visconti). Shirley Hazzard recalls it as 'a staple of British bookcases for generations',[23] but few others even give the impression of having read it, so that a modern reader, perhaps expecting something along the lines of a romantic adventure in the mould of Dumas or Anthony Hope, might be taken aback by the novel's venom and ferocity that seem closer to the atmosphere of Jacobean tragedy or a pre-Renaissance version of *The Godfather*. Set in the Italy of 1360, it is a tortured and involved tale of political treachery and ambition, and familial love and hate: the key word of the text is 'betrayal' and the most pervasive motif is poison. It is a work of impressive descriptive power, as in the villain Visconti's musing about his betrothed that, compared to his sister, she 'was a candle beside the sun'; or in the account of his death at the end of the novel where 'a flock of startled doves flew back in panic, a rainbow of colour; flew so low and so close to de Lana as to blind him for a moment with the whirr of their wings...' However, the quality that seems to have caught Greene's imagination is its precocious pessimism, its dark vision of life and human nature as a constant cycle of deceit and disillusionment: even Visconti is struck by the irony in the phrase 'the promise of the day' ('Hath it ever struck thee how that promise is never fulfilled?'). Greene claimed to recognise and identify with character – equivalents from his own childhood: a noble hero, della Scala, who renounces honour for personal happiness but who fails even at that; a charismatic villain with a genius for evil ('his name was Carter', wrote Greene, relating Visconti to his own school experience[24]). Yet he also admired a fundamental truth, as he saw it, in the book's handling of the pendulum of fate, the way doom hovers to strike even over success: the novel's ending is superb in this regard. Indeed he described the book in such a way that one can see how he tried to transfer its atmosphere into his own work. 'She had given me my pattern,' he wrote, 'perfect evil walking the world where perfect good can never walk again, and only the pendulum ensures that after all in the end justice is done.'[25] Is there a better description of the world and atmosphere of novels like *A Gun for Sale* or *Brighton Rock*?

There was one other special ingredient that he took from Marjorie Bowen and that he obtained from no other writer to the same degree: namely, the intoxicating sense that writing could be fun. For all their massive gifts, this is not something readily communicated by masters such as Henry James, leaving poor Alec Guinness dizzy and breathless trying to follow the sentence structure of *Wings of the Dove*, or Joseph Conrad, labouring for four days over the last sentence of *Heart of Darkness*. There is an exuberance about Bowen's storytelling that overrides the ominousness of the story she has to tell. In this, she had given Greene a map to follow.

'I think it was Miss Bowen's apparent zest that made me want to write,' he reflected. 'One could not read her without believing that to write was to live and to enjoy.' He added ruefully: 'Before one had discovered one's mistake, it was too late ...'[26]

3
The Greene Routine

At the moment when one writes, one is what one is, and the damage
of a lifetime ... cannot be repaired at the moment of composition.
– T.S. Eliot[1]

The moment comes to every writer worth consideration when he
faces for the first time something which he *knows* he cannot do.
It is the moment by which he will be judged, the moment when his
individual technique will be evolved. For technique is more than
anything else a means of evading the personally impossible, of
disguising deficiency.
– Graham Greene[2]

How did Greene write his novels? By the 1930s he had established
a writing routine that he was to stick to for the best part of his life.
He would get up in the morning around 6.30 a.m. and write for two
hours. He would write 500 words – in old age, this was reduced to
300 – and he would count them carefully in the margin as he wrote.
When he reached the requisite number, he would stop, however well
the writing was going. He wrote always by hand in tiny, almost illegible
handwriting on large foolscap. This prevailed until *Travels With My
Aunt*, whose looser, more open structure seemed to demand unlined
sheets: it was written on plain typing paper. According to one of the
closest friends of his final years, Father Leopoldo Duran, he had
a favourite kind of pen he would use: an extra-fine blue-black Japanese
ballpoint.

Anyone who has seriously attempted to write will know how important such rituals and even superstitions are to a writer. The film director Richard Lester once said that he almost walked out of Fred Zinnemann's film, *Julia* (1977) because of a moment when Jane Fonda, who plays Lillian Hellman, becomes so frustrated with her writing (she is trying to finish *The Children's Hour*) that she throws her typewriter out of the window. 'No writer that I have ever met in my whole life – or would ever expect to meet – would ever throw their typewriter out of a window,' Lester said. 'It would be worse than throwing their child out of a window ... All the writers I know, they've got their toys and their tricks and the right pen and they've got to sit there and they've got their mittens on and that's it, that's all part of how they write.'[3] The implements you use, a settled routine, are absolutely essential. (Oscar Wilde would tell of a particularly successful morning's writing when, as he said, 'I put in a comma.' When he was asked what he did in the afternoon, he said with satisfaction: 'I took it out.') I daresay many writers on Greene have attempted to follow the same regime because it seems both seductive and productive. For one thing, it is such a short working day. As his friend, Michael Meyer recalled, he would often pass Graham on the way to the bathroom at 9 a.m., having just got up at the time Graham was finishing work for the day. Also it seemed to offer the prospect of a book being finished in nine months. Having worked with Greene on his film version of *Loser Takes All* and seen the method in action, director Ken Annakin has recorded how he rigorously followed that discipline when writing the screenplay for *Those Magnificent Men in their Flying Machines* (1965).[4] One of Greene's most notable deviations from the formula came after he had returned from Mexico in 1938 and, under the influence of benzedrine, wrote *The Confidential Agent* in six weeks in the mornings whilst working on *The Power and the Glory* in the afternoons. The toll on his temper and his marriage was heavy, and it is not surprising that he can barely remember writing it. 'Each day,' he said, 'I sat down to work with no idea of what turn the plot might take ...'[5]

In fact, it seems that Greene anyway did not pre-plan his novels in great detail. He would have a broad outline in his mind, perhaps a main theme and some main events but, for the most part, he was one of those novelists who write their novels in order to find out how they end. He also always claimed that he did not set out to search for material, that the theme or situation would come to him and could develop out of something quite tiny. An example of this would be *The Third Man*, which he claimed basically developed out of a single sentence written on the back of an envelope (that envelope would be a real collector's item now...) about someone who has attended his friend's funeral only to see him a week later passing by without a sign of recognition.[6]

As is well known, Greene was in the habit of jotting down his dreams with a view to using them in some way in his fiction. (A book recording some of these dreams, *A World of My Own: A Dream Diary* was published in 1992 after his death.) As Cedric Watts has wryly remarked, Greene was so shrewd a literary businessman that he could make money from his sleep. But dreams did have some creative significance for Greene as a writer for, like one of his famous distant relatives, Robert Louis Stevenson with his story of Doctor Jekyll and Mr Hyde, the inspiration for some of his novels came from dreams. Greene's companion over the last thirty years of his life, Yvonne Cloetta, claimed the idea for *It's A Battlefield* and for *The Honorary Consul* came to him in a dream; and Greene said he dreamt Querry's dream in *A Burnt-Out Case* and it helped him at a crucial stage when he was blocked in the narrative. He also kept a diary on long journeys because of what he regarded as his poor memory. This came partly from his experience of writing *The Heart of the Matter* and regretting that he had not kept a journal about his life in West Africa.[7]

As most writers would confirm, however, the most painful part of the process is not getting the idea nor even the initial writing but the reading over and revision. 'Having seen the scrawled and crossed out words on the yellow legal paper he used,' wrote writer and film-maker Bryan Forbes about him, 'I know that he struggled as we all struggle despite the final result appearing effortless.'[8] His friend, Michael Meyer once observed that 'every good writer I have known hates the actual process of writing: Orwell did, so does Greene. I know one or two bad ones who enjoy it...'[9] (This recalls one of the spiky aphorisms of the great Hollywood writer-director, Billy Wilder: 'Show me someone who enjoys writing and I'll show you a bad writer. This does not mean, of course, that everyone who doesn't enjoy writing is a good writer...') Greene would re-read his work during the day, between four and five in the afternoon, partly so it would allow his subconscious to range freely over it during the night when he slept. He would read his words aloud to himself, testing his sentences for assonance, rhythm and flow: possibly the reason why the novels seem so fluent and readable. The acid question always remained: how do you know it is any good? In *A Sort of Life*, by which time he had been writing novels for forty years, Greene confessed that 'even today, until I have passed a quarter of the course, I am uncertain whether I will be able to reach the end'.[10]

Greene had different analogies for the novel-writing process. In *A Sort of Life*, he compares the novelist to a spy: 'he watches, he overhears, he seeks motives and analyses character, and in his attempt to serve literature, he is unscrupulous'.[11] But this was not the only comparison that came to mind. In his book, *Graham Greene: Friend and Brother*, Father Leopoldo Duran quoted Greene as drawing an analogy between writing a novel and piloting a plane: the difficult task is getting the thing launched but once in the air, so to speak, things take on a life of their own and the pilot/author is then just required to guide the craft to its destination and ensure a safe, or at least appropriate, landing. 'A novel is a work in which characters interrelate,' Greene told Duran. 'It doesn't need a plot.'[12]

These observations can be usefully applied to specific novels. For example, in *England Made Me*, Greene took exception to one critic's observation that the characters never evolved, replying that this constriction of character was part of the novel's design – an essential way of expressing the unspoken but traumatic and frustrated incestuous love between Anthony and Kate.[13] But elsewhere he did acknowledge that, when writing a novel, there is invariably one character who refuses to come to life, however hard you try, someone who seems there only for the sake of the story; and that, in the case of *England Made Me*, it was the financier Krogh.[14] I would link that to something Greene says in *A Sort of Life*: that 'a writer's knowledge of himself, realistic and unromantic, is like a store of energy on which he must draw for a lifetime. One volt of it, properly directed, will bring a character alive'.[15] The problem with Krogh, then, is that there is just nothing of Greene in him, nothing to which the author can really relate, so the character remains inert. By contrast, the character of Minty in the same novel (who is only there as a supporting character foil to the hero, a fellow-Englishman who can see through his phoney tie) springs instantly before us – this sly, pathetic Anglo-Catholic down on his luck and going to seed in a foreign land and keeping a spider under his glass as his way of playing God with another creature. Greene's fingerprints are all over Minty: he could have been created by no one else. The problem there is a structural one. Minty's role is purely functional and Greene unwittingly gives him more life than the novel strictly requires, with the result that he tends to upstage the main characters. (Coincidentally, this is exactly what happens too in Peter Duffell's superb 1972 film version of *England Made Me* when Michael Hordern's Minty enters the film: he takes it over.)

When one thinks of Greene's deserved reputation as a story-teller, it is interesting that, in the aforementioned chapter in the Leopoldo Duran book ('The Writer at Work'), he plays down the importance of plot: a novel does not need one, he says. This might sound heretical, but I have never thought plotting to be one of Greene's great strengths. He can lead you on sentence by sentence and page by page through his evocation of character and place, and through his taut psychological analysis and lucid style but sometimes, on sober reflection, the narrative in terms of cause and effect does not always add up. As a psychological thriller with spiritual overtones, *Brighton Rock* is a great novel, but I have always thought the Kolly Kibber business and the alibi of the card under the tablecloth a bit cumbersome; and the detective work of Ida Arnold has always struck me as implausible, where the sleuthing of Miss Marple has been married incongruously to the sexual swagger of Mae West. Nevertheless, the characters, the sinister world they inhabit and their compelling moral dilemmas override such considerations and drive the narrative forward. Similar is the case with *The Third Man*. In his account of the mammoth story conferences he and Carol Reed shared with the great Hollywood mogul, David Selznick, Greene tended to poke fun at Selznick's nitpicking over the plot: in his benzedrine-driven state, which Greene would well understand from his experience of writing *The Confidential Agent*, Selznick at one conference apparently even confused *The Third Man* with a different film entirely.[16] Yet there are occasions in that film where one feels Selznick might have had a point. For all it is a great cinematic moment, it is never entirely clear to me why Harry Lime reappears when he does. Where is he going? To see Anna? But by this time he is not interested in Anna: indeed he is safer if she continues to think he is dead. Why does he walk so unsuspectingly into that final trap? The larger question, though, is: in the end, does it matter? Is not Greene correct: that the interrelationship between the characters is more important and compelling than the overall coherence of the plot? After all, as has been amply demonstrated, *Othello* and *King Lear* have their flaws of narrative credibility: they nevertheless endure as great poetic tragedies.

Another interesting example is *The End of the Affair*. I have sometimes mischievously wondered where the novel might be if the heroine Sarah had not kept a diary. She has to, in narrative terms, not only for character revelation but also out of plot necessity imposed on Greene by the narrative point of view. (The inspiration for the character, Catherine Walston kept a diary which might have validated the device in Greene's mind, but the key issue is whether it seems plausible in terms of the novel.) Because Bendrix is the first-person narrator, it is the only way he can discover what happened to her, but it still seems a rather clumsy narrative device of a kind that great artists are sometimes obliged to adopt to dig themselves out of a plot hole, as in those films of Ingmar Bergman where major narrative revelations hinge on someone's not sealing a letter or sending it to the wrong person. The diary device in *The End of the Affair* is made worse by the ease with which the private detective Parkis is able to find and steal it to give to Bendrix: even for a novel that deals in miracles, this seems far-fetched. Evelyn Waugh was one reader who opined that surely the journal would have been missed. When he was planning his scripts with his scriptwriters, Alfred Hitchcock used to make a distinction between 'coincidental' plotting and 'convenient' plotting: coincidence was acceptable because life can surprise you like that, but not convenience, because that connotes lazy structuring. Sarah's journal strikes me as a bit 'convenient'.

Paradoxically, though, I also think that the way the story is told in that novel is one of the most interesting things about it. In *Ways of Escape*, Greene said that the novel which particularly influenced him here in terms of narrative presentation was Dickens's *Great Expectations*.[17] He was not a great Dickens fan generally, but he was enormously impressed by the way that novel used the first-person narrative whilst still succeeding in including wide varieties of tone, colour and irony. There is a nice, narrative trick that both of them use. The hero is narrating one story in which he seems to be the central character and determining the outcome, at which point something seismic happens and he comes to realise there has been an entirely different story going on from the one he thought he controlled. Thinking that first-person narrative would be a technical advantage as it would obviate the need of deviation (and he had shining examples such as Browning and Henry James before him), Greene actually found it very difficult to handle. He felt particularly it was leading to a monotony of tone – either that of possessive love or obsessive hate – which was one of the main reasons for the inclusion of Parkis and his boy: not so much for plot purposes but simply to get more comedy and common humanity into the text. And although the first-person narration sometimes strains credulity with regard to its presentation of Sarah, it also accumulates great force. The effect of absorbing the heroine's journal into the hero's stream of pain is to make her voice become a part of his consciousness – the woman within, if you like, who is angry with him. She becomes his conscience. For all the element of narrative contrivance, the first-person perspective valuably preserves an intensity of focus.

In talking about Greene's routines as a novel-writer and his evolving technique of craftsmanship as he learns from the successes and failures of others and of himself, I am aware that there is an ultimate mystery about the creative process: as he wrote, not everyone has a book in him or her. That is to say, we could all religiously put into practice the advice and wisdom Greene bequeathed about the writing of novels and still not have the gift to write anywhere near as well as him nor perhaps even the stamina to keep going. There is something unique about him that cannot be duplicated. Something of that is conveyed in the Eliot epigraph that opens this chapter: 'When one writes, one is what one is.' You can have all the technique in the world but, at the point of composition, you are writing out of who and what you are.

When Bryan Forbes visited Greene in his apartment building in Antibes, he was struck by the absence of ornamentation or ostentation. It was, as he put it, 'the habitat of a writer who had few material wants, but who demanded no distractions while he worked'.[18] It is easy to see the writer's living quarters as a correlative to the way he wrote. Eliot once described William Blake's style as 'an extraordinary labour of simplification' and Greene's can be seen in the same way. Father Duran in this context quoted the prayer of Tolstoy which he felt had also been answered in the case of Greene: 'O God, grant me simplicity of style.'[19] Once having arrived at his mature style, he did not show off. He could do the complexities of modernism and stream-of-consciousness – he demonstrated that in *England Made Me* – but it was not where his talent or interest principally lay. It was not him. At the moment when one writes, one is what one is. If asked to define what that was in the case of Greene, I would be drawn to Roberto Rossellini's comment about Charlie Chaplin after seeing his 1957 film, *A King in New York*, the idea for which I have always thought came from Greene:[20] 'It is the work of a truly free man.' Greene's achievement has this same sense of individuality, fearlessness and freedom. As Forbes (1992) put it: 'He was willing to share his knowledge of the world, fight for lost causes, while, at the same time, pursuing without compromise his chosen craft.'[21]

4
Greene on the Screen

When I describe a scene I capture it with the moving eye of the cine-camera rather than with the photographer's eye – which leaves it frozen. In this precise domain I think the cinema has influenced me.

Authors like Walter Scott or the Victorians were influenced by paintings and constructed their backgrounds as though they were static and came from the hands of a Constable. I work with a camera, following my characters and their movements. So the landscape moves. When I turn my head and look at the harbour, my head moves, the houses move, the boats move, don't they?

– Graham Greene[1]

One thing the films had taught the eye, Savory thought, the beauty of the landscape in motion, how a church tower moved behind and above the trees, how it dipped and soared with the uneven human stride, the loveliness of a chimney rising towards a cloud and sinking behind the further cowls. That sense of movement must be conveyed in prose...

– Graham Greene, *Stamboul Train*, Part Three.

No major writer of the twentieth century has had a deeper involvement – personally and professionally, critically and creatively – with the cinema than Graham Greene. He has been a film critic, screenwriter, screenplay adaptor, script doctor, letter-writer on matters cinematic and even film actor. Moreover virtually every fictional word he ever wrote has been adapted for either film or television, one of the few exceptions being *It's A Battlefield*, which Greene thought, ironically enough, was one of the most cinematic things he had ever written and had even been composed with this in mind. The cinema impinged on Greene's personal life in incidental but significant ways: its impingement on his creative development was, I believe, crucial. In terms of the material he supplied and created, Greene gave a lot to the cinema. In terms of its impact and influence on his work, the cinema gave as much, if not more, to Greene.

A significant reference to the cinema occurs in the very first paragraph of the first chapter of the autobiography of *A Sort of Life*. He recalls how his father, who was the then headmaster of Berkhamsted High School, had allowed his senior boys to attend a screening of the first *Tarzan* film under the mistaken impression that it was an educational movie of some anthropological use and interest. Thereafter, Greene noted wryly, his father 'regarded the cinema with a sense of disillusion and suspicion'.[2] It is an amusing anecdote but one with some resonance. The inference could be drawn (it would certainly not be out of character) that Greene's early attraction to the cinema was partly an act of rebellion against his upbringing.

There is another personal connection one might make between Greene and the cinema in that it was through his film reviewing that he met his wife Vivien Dayrell-Browning. Writing in *The Oxford Outlook* in February 1925, he had begun his article on 'The Average Film' as follows: 'We are most of us nowadays considerably over-sexed. We either go to the Church and worship the Virgin Mary or to a public house and snigger over stories and limericks; and this exaggeration of the sex instinct has had a bad effect on art, on the cinematograph as well as on the stage.'[3] Vivien had written to him, pulling him up on his second line, suggesting that 'venerate' was more appropriate than 'worship': interesting that their first contact was over a theological dispute over Catholic terminology. (Greene was not a Catholic at this time, of course.) Greene wrote a courteous apology and proposed a meeting: they fell in love. Apparently he took her to see a Garbo film on one of their first dates, and, as Sherry (1989) has shown, a number of Greene's early letters to Vivien are about his film tastes: how he hates Rudolph Valentino but likes Douglas Fairbanks. He would tell her of films he was looking forward to seeing, such as Alfred Hitchcock's *The Lodger* (1926), with Ivor Novello as a suspected

Jack the Ripper. He kept up his cinema-going habit when he was subeditor on the *Nottingham Journal*, and although he liked the communal nature of the cinema – something he was to develop in his later criticism – he also liked sneaking into the cinema on his own (a situation which would ominously feature in a short story such as 'A Little Place Off the Edgware Road' in 1939). It was not simply relaxation: it seemed to release an imaginative energy. Going to the cinema, he would say, put him in the mood for creative work.[4] Interestingly, when he became a regular film critic in the 1930s, he was also to find it a release but in a slightly different way: it was an escape from writing fiction – from what he called 'that hellish problem of construction in Chapter 6, from the secondary character who obstinately refused to come alive, escape for an hour and a half from the melancholy which falls inexorably round the novelist when he has lived for too many months on end in his private world'.[5] What is interesting also about this early enthusiasm is the revelation about wishing to be involved in the making of films as well as simply seeing them and criticising them. In 1927 he was writing to Vivien: 'Apart from marrying you, I think the most wonderful thing in the world would be to write and produce a really first-class film – something as good as Manon Lescaut. Oo!'[6] What would he have thought, one wonders, over the poll in 1999 organised by the British Film Institute to determine the greatest British film of the century, which was to be won by *The Third Man*? That surely would have been the realisation of his dream.

Much of Greene's earliest published writing was in the form of reviews or articles about the cinema. As an undergraduate, when he became editor of *The Oxford Outlook* in 1924, he appointed himself as occasional film critic. The criticism is notable not simply because of its expression of opinion on individual films but the sense it gives of a young man reflecting on the expressive potential of a young art. Thus, when reviewing Arthur Robison's *Warning Shadows* in June 1925, he hopes that the gulf between naturalism and impressionism – by which he means the self-effacement of the American style and the stylised expressionism of the German – can be brought in closer proximity: one will see this mixture in his own fiction, in *Brighton Rock*, in *The Ministry of Fear*, where a naturalistic landscape will become charged with extremities of menace. In his first film article for *The Times* (9 April 1928), he talks of the clumsiness of words in comparison with the imagistic brilliance of a cinematic master like Chaplin in *A Woman of Paris* (1923), who can convey the anguish of a jilted fiancée at a railway station simply through the play of shadow on her face; or like Erich von Stroheim in *Greed* (1924), who implies the lovers' passion and self-absorption simply through a shot of their backs and their imperviousness to the wild, natural elements around them. 'The object of the film,' he declares in the same review, 'should be the translation of thought back into images'.[7] He will go on to write equally thoughtful pieces about rhythm in film, the use of sound and silence (spurred here by the advent of talkies) and an aesthetic of film that would draw a keen distinction between it and drama. It would be hard to find any other English critic at the time grappling so seriously with the expressive vocabulary of the cinema in a manner that recalls some of the early pioneers of film aesthetics, such as Hugo Munsterberg and Vachel Lindsay, not to mention Sergei Eisenstein. It seems therefore an entirely logical progression that he should suggest himself as film critic of *The Spectator* to their Literary Editor, Derek Vershoyle, at a cocktail party after what he memorably called 'the dangerous third martini'.[8] He would always claim that his style as a writer was less influenced by writing for the cinema than by watching films.

Between 1935 and 1940, as the film critic of *The Spectator* and co-editor of the monthly periodical *Night and Day* for whom he also wrote on the cinema, he reviewed well over 400 films. His collected writings on film – and this would exclude his actual screenplays – is more voluminous than his collected short stories and, by any criterion, is an important dimension of Greene's curriculum vitae. Unlike George Orwell, say, who also reviewed film for a time in the 1930s but who really had very little interest or feeling for the cinema (in contrast to Greene's experience with the third dangerous martini, Orwell at press receptions always felt he was being asked to sell his soul for a glass of inferior sherry[9]), Greene took film reviewing seriously and had a deservedly high reputation. 'The best critic we had,' was the verdict on him of Britain's founding father of documentary, John Grierson in *The Spectator*; Alistair Cooke was to include him in his personal anthology of the best film criticism of the 1930s, *Garbo and the Night Watchmen*;[10] and a young Dilys Powell was to say that Greene was her model when she started out as a film critic. 'It struck me that this was the kind of thing that film criticism should be,' she wrote.

'He liked the silent films, he liked the old popular films, but he also had an instinctive reaction to what was new or what was not so traditional. One was terribly grateful that somebody of his literary genius should care so much and with such deep and original feeling about a medium that was not literary, which is partly visual and partly literary.'[11]

Nowadays Greene's contribution to film criticism is probably best remembered through his notorious review in *Night and Day* (28 October 1937) of John Ford's film, *Wee Willie Winkie*, which seemed to be implying that its child star, Shirley Temple was a sexually provocative midget procured by Twentieth Century Fox for immoral purposes and which culminated in a successful prosecution for libel against the journal. (Curiously his review of the Shirley Temple film, *Captain January* in the previous year, which elicited no reaction, seems to me every bit as provocative: describing the film as 'decadent' and 'depraved', he suggests that some of the moppet's popularity 'seems to rest on a coquetry quite as mature as Miss Colbert's and on an oddly precocious body as voluptuous in grey flannel trousers as Miss Dietrich's'.[12]) The review may have had far-reaching implications. Philip French once suggested to me that John Ford's version of *The Power and the Glory*, a very free adaptation entitled *The Fugitive* (1947) and one of Ford's worst received films, might have been the director's revenge on Greene for his *Wee Willie Winkie* review. The first inklings of American suspicion of Greene as a potentially undesirable alien might also stem from that review, with its satirically salacious mockery of one of their national treasures, particularly as only three weeks earlier, in a review of James Whale's film, *The Road Back*, he had savaged America's tendency to see everything in its own image. 'What use in pretending that with these allies it was ever possible to fight for civilization?' he sneered. 'For Mother's Day, yes, for anti-vivisection and humanitarianism, the pet dog and the home fire, for the coed college and the campus. Civilisation would shock them: eyes on the guidebook for safety, they pass it quickly as if it were a nude in a national collection.'[13] This punchy, if patronising, polemic is one of the earliest manifestations of Greene's anti-Americanism that was to become even more marked and controversial in his later years.

This polemic is also an indicator of how cruel his criticism could be. In his anthology of Greene's writings on the cinema, *Mornings in the Dark* (1993), David Parkinson has given some examples of how this barbed wit extended to performers he did not like, on whom he indulged his propensity for animal imagery. Greta Garbo is famously likened to an Arab mare; Herbert Marshall reminds him of a 'large, sentimental, moulting dog', which 'confirms one's preference for cats'; and Irene Dunne is distinguished from the farm horse to which she sings in Rouben Mamoulian's *High, Wide and Handsome* (1937) as 'the one without the white patch on her forehead'.[14] Reviewing William Keighley's gangster movie, *Bullets or Ballots* (*The Spectator*, 27 November 1936), he comments that Edward G. Robinson's mouth is 'more than ever like the long flat slit in a pillar box'. The pugnacity is worthy of Robinson himself and certainly fulfils one of the critical criteria he enumerated in his article 'What is Criticism?' for the Autumn 1936 issue of *Sight and Sound*: namely, that 'the critic, as much as the film, is supposed to entertain'.

Yet it is in this article that the essential seriousness of Greene's attitude to the cinema, which Dilys Powell so valued, also becomes apparent. 'One need not deny to either books or films of popular middle-class entertainment a useful social service,' he writes, 'as long as it is recognised that social service has nothing to do with the art of cinema or the art of fiction. What I object to is the idea that it is the *critic's* business to assist films to fulfil a social function. The critic's business should be confined to the art.' A little later on, he disparages the traditional cinema reviewer for an account of a film that is usually a lightweight amalgam of narrative and gossip instead of what should be the reviewer's concern, which Greene says, is 'the film as a film, that is to say, a sequence of photographs arranged in a certain way to get a certain effect'.[15] As a formulation of the film critic's task, it is remarkable how similar that is to Robin Wood's definition of correct cinematic critical procedure in his pioneering book on Alfred Hitchcock thirty years later, where the critics' task is defined as 'to look without preconceptions at the sequence of images that [the director] gives us and consider their first-hand response to those images'.[16] (Along with Wood, another of the critics for the magazine *Movie*, V.F. Perkins was to call his book on film aesthetics, *Film as Film*, an echo of Greene's insistence that critics should concern themselves with 'the film as a film'.) Indeed it is remarkable how, even in the abbreviated forms of reviews and articles, he anticipates some of the foremost future film theorists in his ideas. In his attack on Robert Flaherty's manipulation of reality in *Man of Aran*, he anticipated a similar criticism that the great French film theorist André Bazin was to make of the montage fakery of Flaherty's *Louisiana Story* (1948). Indeed, when Greene expresses a wariness of montage that would 'keep the mind at too high a tension...not allowing for the non-vital moments of life to be shown',[17] he is anticipating an important aspect of the aesthetics of Bazin, who, like Greene, thought the art of the cinema lay less in the manipulation of reality through montage and more in an artistic vision that respected the natural world but enabled us to see it in a fresh way. What might have connected them here indeed was not just aestheticism but Catholicism. Describing Bazin's mistrust of montage, Conrad (2000) suggested that he 'considered it heretical, because it manipulated and rearranged a reality ordained – according to Bazin's Catholic mysticism – by God'.[18]

There are other ways also in which Greene's literary and artistic personality are to be anticipated by his film criticism. Even his dislike of the new developments in Technicolor – or 'technihorror', as he called it – is expressed in a very revealing example. Reviewing the innovative colour photography in Rouben Mamoulian's *Becky Sharp* (1935), he takes leave to query whether Technicolor can reproduce with sufficient accuracy 'the suit that has been worn too long, the oily hat'[19]: how typical that he should criticise it for failing to pick up seediness. When he admires Julien Duvivier's use in *Un Carnet De Bal* of what he calls the 'evil detail' and his reference to a style where 'the camera shoots at a slant so that the dingy flat rears like a sinking ship',[20] one has an extraordinary anticipation of Greene's own future work in the cinema, notably his collaborations with Carol Reed. For the use of 'evil detail', think only of the pet snake being flushed down the toilet in *The Fallen Idol* or, in the same film, the hairslide dropping like a fat black spider on the pillow of the sleeping boy to announce the deranged presence of Mrs Baines (an image, incidentally, inspired directly from the Greene short story on which it is based, 'The Basement Room'). For a film with a style where 'the camera shoots at a slant', the immediate and inevitable example that would spring to any cineaste's mind would be *The Third Man*, where Carol Reed's deployment of distorted camera angles suggests a world out of joint and morality awry.[21]

In his essay 'Subjects and Stories', published in *Footnotes to the Film* in 1937, Greene set out two important planks of his cinematic credo:

their significance is in the fact that they could be part of Greene's overall artistic credo as a writer. The first was his embrace of the cinema's popularity. 'The cinema has got to appeal to millions,' he wrote, 'we have got to accept its popularity as a virtue, not turn away from it as a vice'. Idealistic about the potential of the cinema, he believed an audience wanted not to be soothed but excited: 'if you excite your audience first, you can put over what you will of horror, suffering, truth'.[22] And in musing on the proper popular use of film that seems to pulse with the same blood as its audience, Greene rejects the 'pompous themes the censor denies us' and also works that reflect tepid middle-class virtues in favour of the common-life vitality of the thriller. 'And when we have attained to a more popular drama,' he writes, 'even if it is in the simplest terms of blood on a garage floor…, the scream of cars in flight, all the old excitements at their simplest and most sure-fire, then we can begin – secretly, with low cunning – to develop our poetic drama.'[23] Even while he is extolling there the cinematic art that belongs not to the ivory tower but to nasty, brutish, short, natural life, he is surely also defining the way his own novels were developing. It is a blueprint for *Brighton Rock*.

The second plank of Greene's cinematic credo is hinted at in the last phrase of the preceding quotation: 'poetic drama'. In the first paragraph of the essay, he quotes a comment of Chekhov about his fellow Russian writers that for Greene is (and remained) the finest statement of the theme of the artist: 'The best of them are realistic and paint life as it is, but because every line is permeated, as with a juice, by awareness of a purpose, you feel, besides life as it is, also life as it ought to be, and this captivates you.'[24] For Greene, this was the goal of the cinema too, and he glimpsed that ideal in material as diverse as Fritz Lang's *Fury* (1936), the social comedies of Frank Capra and René Clair, Laurel and Hardy, the Marx Brothers in *Duck Soup* (1932), the early films of Carol Reed (anticipating their future collaboration) and in Chaplin, whose 'few simple ideas' – 'courage, loyalty, labour: against the same nihilistic background of purposeless suffering' – he likened to those of Conrad.[25] In 'Stories and Subjects', he appropriates for his own cinematic purposes Ford Madox Ford's definition of the poetic writer: 'not the power melodiously to arrange words but the power to suggest human values'; and one is struck there by how similar that is to the way Lindsay Anderson used to talk of Humphrey Jennings and John Ford as 'poetic directors'. Like Bazin, Greene seems to be looking in films for what he might term the poetry of the everyday. When talking of the sense of moral values present in Duvivier's *Pépé le Moko* and *Un Carnet De Bal*, he uses the resonant phrase 'poetic realism', which, to my knowledge, was not used in English film criticism before Greene but became a way of defining a whole tradition of distinguished 1930s French cinema that was to be one of the influences on the film noir of Hollywood in the next decade.[26] Life as it is, and life as it ought to be: art arising from the creator's vision of the simultaneity of those two things, and the tension, oscillation, conflict, contradiction and connection between them. In his perceptiveness and in his percipience, Greene can fairly be regarded as one of the most important film critics of his time.

But if Greene's contribution to the cinema was enormous (and his own screenplays and film adaptations of his work will be considered at a later stage), what he learnt from the cinema seems to me crucial for his future development as a writer. Clearly the commercial element comes in here. He was paid £1738. 3s 8d by Twentieth Century Fox for the screen rights to *Stamboul Train* which they were to make as *Orient Express*; and it was essentially his film earnings that enabled him to leave his job at Eyre & Spottiswoode in 1948, where he had been a part-time editor and full-time managing director, encouraging the publication among others of Mauriac and Narayan. For this reason he tended to be fairly relaxed about film versions of his novels, some of which he rubbished without actually having seen them. He believed, along with Andre Bazin, that a bad film of a good book does not really harm the book and the measure of financial security he obtained from selling the rights enabled him to continue writing. But the real impact of the cinema is on the style itself:

> Suddenly, as the wind took the snow and blew it aside, a cart appeared in the gap ten yards away and right in front of them. Myatt had just time to see the bemused eyes of the oxen, to calculate where their horns would smash the glass of the windscreen: an elderly man screamed and dropped his goad and jumped. The driver wrenched his wheel round, the car leapt a bank, rode crazily on two wheels, while the others hummed and revolved between the wind and earth, leant farther and farther over till Myatt could see the ground rise like boiling milk, left the bank, touched two

wheels to the ground, touched four, and roared down the road at sixty-five miles an hour, while the snow closed behind them, and hid the oxen and cart and the astonished terrified old man.

'Drive slower,' Myatt gasped, but the driver turned and grinned at him and waved an untrembling hand.

That passage from Chapter 3 of Part 4 of *Stamboul Train* is a good example of the dynamic style that Greene had adopted and which he had absorbed from watching films. As indicated in the first epigraph to this chapter, Greene now thought of description in a novel in terms of a moving camera, something active, not static. As an example of that, one need only look at the opening paragraph of *The Power and the Glory*, with its superb sweeping aerial view of the Mexican setting as a few vultures look down disdainfully at Tench before one of them flies off and flaps across the town towards the sea. Dialogue in a novel should not be exposition but 'a form of action, with the quickness of action'[27]; it was something that John Huston, the most literary and literate of all the great Hollywood masters, also practised. He was writing action novels and action 'can only be expressed by a subject, a verb and an object, perhaps a rhythm – little else. Even an adjective slows the pace or tranquillises the nerve'.[28] One can see that dramatically at work in the above extract from *Stamboul Train*: even when adjectives are used ('astonished terrified old') the deliberate absence of punctuation keeps the momentum of the passage going. 'Excitement is a situation,' he wrote. 'It mustn't be wrapped up in thoughts, similes, metaphors.'[29]

There is only one simile in that passage and it is a magnificent one: the snowy ground rising 'like boiling milk' towards the hero, which adds colour, suddenness and danger to the description. 'The sort of novel I was trying ... was not made with words but with movement, action, character. Discrimination in one's words is certainly required, but not love of one's words – that is a form of self-love ... '[30] And there is hardly a trace of what he was to call 'the beastly adverb – far more damaging to a writer than an adjective'.[31] Much of this, I believe, came from the imbibing of film technique as spectator and critic, and even from the practice of criticism itself, when he had to describe and evoke a sequence that had particularly excited him. One can see this, for example, in his gripping description of the opening of Julien Duvivier's 1935 film, *La Bandera* for *The Spectator*

(6 December 1935), a review that opens as compellingly as one of Greene's own stories. It is even more apparent in his visual evocation of Jean Gabin's fateful final walk in *Pépé le Moko* 'in his glossy shoes and his best muffler down the steep steps to the European town where the Inspector awaits him, the camera trucking down ahead of him registering the happy, crazy stride, the rash, nostalgic impulse'. (*The Spectator*, 23 April 1937) This goes a little beyond evocative criticism: it is a creative writer's response to a scene that has stirred him and straining to do justice to its cinematic imagination through the stark precision of the single adjectives at the beginning ('glossy', 'best', 'steep'); through a sentence structure that mimics the verve and bounce of Gabin's gait; and through the final resounding symmetry of structure that draws together movement and mood ('happy, crazy stride', 'rash, nostalgic impulse'). If, as George Orwell said about his own work, it was the ingredient of political purpose that took the lifelessness out of his novels, in Greene's case it was the ingredient of the cinema that gave an example and impetus to the style of novel he wished to write.

For example, if one wished to define what was meant by describing Greene as a 'cinematic' novelist, one might cite a scene in the opening chapter of Part 5 of *Brighton Rock*.[32] Spicer has been murdered: his girlfriend Sylvie goes out with Pinkie to a nightclub outside Brighton and they go off to have sex in a car park:

> 'Which is your car?' Sylvie said.
> 'That Morris.'
> 'No good to us,' Sylvie said. She darted down the line of cars. 'This Ford.' She pulled the door open, said 'Oh, pardon me,' and shut it, scrambled into the back of the next car in line and waited for him. 'Oh,' her voice softly and passionately pronounced from the dim interior, 'I love a Lancia.' He stood in the doorway and the darkness peeled away between him and the fair vacuous face. Her skirt drawn up above her knees she waited for him with luxurious docility.

What one has here is a sort of cutting sequence: following Sylvie as she darts down the line of cars; a track along the cars; an opening door and a reaction shot of Sylvie as she looks in the car but we are not told what she has seen; the arrival of Pinkie and the equivalent of a point of view shot as he looks at her preparing for him in the car. There is even a discreet but telling indication of lighting. This is the kind of thing Greene learnt from the cinema – from the critical act of watching films – and through it learned what had been going wrong in his early novels and how to put it right.

There are two films which Greene saw during this period which seem to me to have made a particular impact on him and which were to influence his subsequent literary practice. One was Duvivier's *Pepe le Moko*, which he declared 'one of the most exciting and moving films I can recall seeing': it succeeded in 'raising the thriller to a poetic level', which became the specific stylistic aim of the novel he was working on at the time, *Brighton Rock*. The parallelism between the two works can be seen in the strong sense and importance of location (symbolic as well as physical); and the theme of honour amongst thieves, in which a key scene becomes the killing of an informer. Indeed, a lot of the symbolism and general paraphernalia of *Pepe* – fortune tellers and card games, blind beggars and even a potent gramophone record – are to turn up in *Brighton Rock*, not accidentally but suitably transformed for the novelist's purpose. Reviewing the year's films at the end of 1937, he particularly praised *Pépé* and *Carnet de Bal* for their evocation of atmosphere, which he characterised by quoting Marlowe's Mephistopheles in *Doctor Faustus*: 'Why, this is hell nor am I out of it.' In the novel *Brighton Rock*, the seedy villainous lawyer Prewitt, who, like Harry Lime, does not suffer from conscience but from indigestion, quotes the selfsame line to evoke his situation (see Part 7, Chapter 3). This is clearly not coincidental. When Greene was writing the screenplay for the film of *Brighton Rock* in 1947, he asked the Boulting Brothers if they would design the costumes to look like those in *Pepe le Moko* – certainly visually, Nigel Stock's Cubitt could have stepped straight out of the Duvivier film – which suggests the two works were closely connected in his mind. The influence might even have extended to *The Third Man*. In *Pepe*, the documentary shots of the Casbah set the scene in much the same way as Carol Reed's opening shots of Vienna; there is a similar babble of languages and range of nationalities; and Gabin's hero – the charming rogue with an almost supernatural knowledge of the city, whose much-anticipated entrance is tantalisingly delayed until he steps from the shadows, whose downfall occurs when he steps outside the territorial boundaries that he himself has devised – has much in common with the potent presentation of Harry Lime. Greene's film-going there was to feed productively into his own creative work.

The other film from this period that seems to me to have had a profound and far-reaching impact on Greene was the 1936 Samuel Goldwyn production, *These Three*, directed by William Wyler from what Greene called a 'thematically diluted' version of Lillian Hellman's play, *The Children's Hour*. Writing about the film in *The Spectator* of 1 May 1936, Greene declared at the outset that 'I have seldom been so moved by any fictional film.' The movie concerns the way the lives of two schoolteachers are destroyed by the malicious lie of a child. 'Never has childhood been represented so convincingly on the screen, with an authenticity guaranteed by one's own memories,' Greene went on. 'The more than human evil of the lying sadistic child is suggested with shocking mastery by Bonita Glanville... it has enough truth and intensity to stand for the whole of the dark side of childhood, in which the ignorance and weakness of the many allows complete mastery to the few.'[33]

Most of us can date the moment when we first became interested in Greene and unusually perhaps, for me it was the moment when I first read that review thirty years ago on the publication of his film criticism in *The Pleasure Dome*. Because I loved the film and William Wyler was (and remains) my favourite director, I was bowled over by Greene's enthusiasm. But the question it begs now is: why did that film have such an impact on him? What might the review reveal and imply about Greene the man as well as his artistic personality?

From what we now know about Greene's background, it is safe to say that the theme of childhood and its importance in the formation of character was something he related to strongly. The girl's emotional sadism was something Greene vividly recognised from his own experience of being bullied at school. One could take this recognition even further. Later in the review, Greene will talk about a kind of virginal evil that the girl Mary represents which is one of the reasons why it is so shocking; and he is almost equally impressed by the characterisation and performance of the girl Rosalie (played by Marcia Mae Jones) who has the misfortune to fall under Mary's spell. Might this not be a precursor of the Pinkie/Rose relationship in *Brighton Rock*, which, like *These Three*, is not really about right and wrong but about good and evil, where the evil youth is also virginal and often referred to as 'The Boy' (to emphasise the horror of evil in one so young) and where the person in thrall to him is called Rose (in memory perhaps of Rosalie?).

Another thing about *These Three* that might well have stuck in Greene's mind is a central irony in the plotting: namely, that the girl's lie about the teachers (which in the film turns on the allegation that one of the teachers is in love with the other's fiancé) turns out to be true. In the revelation scene, the guilty teacher keeps returning to this point: why did the child pick on the one lie that had the grain of truth? Greene will write the screenplay for the Carol Reed film, *The Fallen Idol* (1948), based on his short story 'The Basement Room', where something similar is going to occur: a child will be placed in a bewildering situation surrounded by accusing adults and, like Rosalie at a key moment in *These Three*, will not know whether to lie or tell the truth to protect the person he wishes to protect and at the same time to protect himself. That *These Three* was in the mind of Greene and Reed when they came to make *The Fallen Idol* seems to me very probable, given the thematic and even compositional similarity between the two films at certain stages, given Greene's admiration of the Wyler film, and given the fact that Carol Reed's favourite director was none other than William Wyler. It is another example of the way Greene absorbed the essence of something he esteemed to transform it at a later time into something akin to the original but also different and personal. I think he loved the idea of the lie that tells the truth: revelation by oblique and even misleading disclosure. It will crop up as a motif in *Our Man in Havana*, as Wormold invents secret agents who then seem dangerously to materialise. It will be Picasso's definition of what art is: Art is a lie that tells the truth.[34]

Greene ceased regular film reviewing in 1940. His connection with the cinema was, of course, to continue, both as a novelist whose work was invariably adapted for the screen and as a screenwriter. (Shelden (1994) has noted how Greene's earnings from film sources soared during the 1940s.[35]) Screen adaptations of Greene's work will be looked at later, as will those other adaptations of his that were not self-adaptations. He himself famously gave a bad review to his own film adaptation of a John Galsworthy story, *Twenty-One Days* (1939), promising never to write for the screen again (*The Spectator*, 12 January 1940): the film is interestingly quoted in Neil Jordan's remake of *The End of the Affair* (1999). He also adapted Otto Preminger's version of George Bernard Shaw's *Saint Joan* (1957), one of the biggest flops in film history but where at least, Greene claimed, there were more jokes than in Shaw's original. Elsewhere he maintained a presence on the periphery of film matters. He was occasionally consulted as a script doctor, most memorably, according to his own account, when he was approached by Sam Zimbalist, producer of the MGM epic, *Ben-Hur* (1959), to help with the film's finale because, Zimbalist said, 'there's a bit of an anticlimax after the Crucifixion'.[36] His friendship with Charlie Chaplin has been mentioned in a previous chapter, particularly his support for him when the latter was in the process of being driven into exile by McCarthyist forces in America, and there were two significant filmic outcomes from this. One was Greene's bequeathing an idea to Chaplin that, as I have argued, was to be developed in *A King in New York*; and his support and encouragement of Chaplin to write his autobiography, which created a sensation when it was published in 1964.[37] Greene's letter to *The New Statesman* (27 September 1952) in support of Chaplin is one of his most potent political interventions in print: 'But the disgrace of an ally is our disgrace ... Intolerance in any country wounds freedom throughout the world.' Elsewhere his political interventions on filmic matters could be more playful, as in a letter to the *Sunday Telegraph* (24 April 1965), where he recommends readers to attend the programme at the Empire Theatre not so much for the main feature, *The Americanisation of Emily* but for the Tom and Jerry cartoon in support (not identified, but almost certainly *The Cat's Me-Ouch*) which Greene proposes is a 'scathing attack on the American policy in Vietnam, and the inability of the Pentagon to understand the nature of guerrilla warfare'. And, as an example of Greene as practical joker, one should mention his appearance as a screen actor (billed as 'Henry Graham', his own forenames) in no less a film than Francois Truffaut's *Day for Night* (1973) playing an English insurance representative.[38]

So the cinema played an important part in Greene's life and work in a variety of different ways. The connection could simply be a commercial one – the sale of film rights could guarantee financial security while he wrote his next novel. It could be a personal one, Greene rewriting the main female part of *Stamboul Train* after being taken with Anna Sten in Feodor Ozep's film, *The Crime of Dmitri Karamazov* (1931).[39] Mainly the connection went to the very roots of Greene's literary inspiration. More than any other twentieth-century writer, he exemplified and embodied the multifarious links between film and fiction – as a cinematic novelist whose every fictional word, virtually, has been visualised; as screenwriter, screen doctor, film actor, film critic whose experience of, and sensitivity to, cinema influenced and invigorated style, theme, characterisation and ideas. For almost all major novelists of the last century, the cinema connection was incidental. For Greene, it was fundamental.

5
Laughter in the Shadow of the Gallows

Castro: According to the estimate of probabilities, you should
         be dead.
Greene: Well, I always was bad at mathematics.[1]

Graham unusually gloomy and depressed – even for Graham.
Catherine Walston, Diary entry, 1949.[2]

When Alfred Hitchcock was coaching the writer Jim Allardyce in the
art of writing those famous droll introductions to his television
shows, he gave him two examples of humour that were to serve him
as a guideline. One was simply his film, *The Trouble With Harry*
(1954), one of his most mordantly comic tales in which the cast
spend most of the time trying to explain or hide Harry's dead body.
(Come to think of it, *The Trouble With Harry* would be a superb
alternative title to *The Third Man*.) The second example was a favourite
Hitchcock joke: about a condemned man who is being led to the gallows
for execution and who, on spotting the trapdoor, turns to his jailer
and murmurs: 'I say – is that thing safe?'

'Laughter in the shadow of the gallows' is a phrase that a Swedish
critic used about *Travels With My Aunt* and which apparently delighted
Greene: he refers to it in his brief introduction to an edition of four of
his favourite novels (the other three being *The Power and the Glory*,
The Quiet American and *The Honorary Consul*). One of the curious
things about Greene's career – and it does seem to be bound up with

events in his own life – is that, as death grows nearer, the books grow not just shorter but funnier. 'I am struck by an odd fact,' he said about his short stories. 'Humour enters very late and unexpectedly. So perhaps the stories which make up the collection, *May We Borrow Your Husband?*, all written during what should have been the last decade of my life, are an escape in humour from the thought of death.' He goes on: 'Writing is a form of therapy: sometimes I wonder how all those who do not write, compose or paint can manage to escape the madness, the melancholia, the panic-fear which is inherent in the human situation.'[3]

Greene lived until he was 86 years old, which is a long time for someone who seems to have thought of suicide fairly regularly from an early age. He had attempted it at public school, at different stages sawing open his knee, eating a tin of hair pomade, drinking a bottle of eye drops and attempting to drown after taking over a dozen aspirins. In his notorious essay 'The Revolver in the Corner Cupboard' and later in *A Sort of Life*, he outlined his teenage attempts at Russian roulette (it is this tale that he is regaling Castro with in the opening epigraph). This has become one of the staples of Greene mythology. Of all the controversies surrounding Michael Shelden's hostile, revisionist biography, perhaps the most contentious was his daring to cast doubt on this story: maybe they were only the caps of starter pistols – which presumably, if pointed at one's skull, could still do a considerable amount of damage. Nevertheless, it has always seemed to me rather like whether George Orwell really did shoot that elephant or whether Alfred Hitchcock really was locked up in a prison cell as a practical joke by a policeman friend of his father when he was a young man that gave him a lasting fear of the police (one of Hitchcock's most assiduous biographers, Donald Spoto could find no evidence that this had actually happened). *The Heart of the Matter is* surely not whether the story is true but the reason that the artist keeps retelling the tale as if it were. If it were demonstrated to be untrue, it seems to me that the story becomes more significant rather than less because it suggests it has an importance in the author's own perception of self: it is giving something away. It is the lie that tells the truth: that conception at the heart of one of Greene's favourite films discussed in the previous chapter, Wyler's *These Three*, an idea that caught Greene's imagination. Whether the Russian roulette story is true or not, what is undeniable is the centrality of the idea of suicide in Greene's life and work. It occurs as a motif in a huge number of his works – *Brighton Rock*, *The Ministry of Fear*, *The Heart of the Matter*, *The Living Room*, *The Complaisant Lover*, *A Burnt-Out Case*, to name but a few. And it runs like a leitmotif in his own life. In 1952, his close friend, Michael Meyer could recall that, when he was musing with Edward Sackville-West what they would all be doing in ten years' time and the subject of Greene came up, Sackville-West said; 'Oh, Graham'll have committed suicide.' And Meyer could remember agreeing with that.[4] Greene's French literary agent, Marie Francoise Allain, who published a superb book-length interview with him, *The Other Man* (1983), remembers seeing him just six months before his death and his commenting about his relationship with Yvonne Cloetta: 'If she didn't exist, I'd put a bullet through my head.'[5]

Greene described himself as a 'manic-depressive' and said that the humour was the manic side of that depression. He was certainly aware that the distance between comedy and tragedy was sometimes paper-thin: that even the most intensely tragic works, from *King Lear* to *Jude the Obscure* veer towards black comedy on occasion; that a writer whom Greene revered, Dostoevsky (there is a moving moment in the third part of the BBC's 1993 *Arena* documentary where Greene is in tears when he visits the Dostoevsky museum in Moscow) was fond of creating scenes where the psychological torments of characters are counterpointed by the laughter of onlookers to whom the suffering looks merely funny. (I am thinking particularly of scenes in *Crime and Punishment* involving Sonia's father and mother.) Greene's great friend, Charlie Chaplin had a simple formula for screen direction: 'Long shot for comedy; close-up for tragedy,' as if the only fundamental difference between them were distance and point of view. So, if Greene's later work veers more towards comedy, this does not necessarily mean that his themes are any the less serious or even that he has changed that much: it is just that his artistic and temperamental *strategies* have shifted to accommodate the 'panic-fear'. The turning point, I think, occurred with his tortured and tremendous novel, written at the end of a traumatic decade for him, *A Burnt-Out Case* (1961), the bleakest he ever wrote, which teeters throughout not only on the verge of self-portrait but also of self-parody. 'My last bout of depression, my worst, I think,' Greene told Marie-Francois Allain, 'coincided with the gestation of *A Burnt-Out Case*'.[6] What was not noticed by critics at the time, Greene remarked slyly, was that 'in the course of the blackest book I have written I had discovered Comedy.'[7]

In his early novels and stories, the comedy tends to be incidental more than central. There is an interesting epigraph to his first big success, *Stamboul Train* (1932), where he quotes Santanyana: 'Everything in nature is lyrical in its ideal essence: tragic in its fate: and comic in its existence.' However, it is only in the later works that this will come through. The humour in early Greene tends either to be grim (like the vultures' eye-view of the dentist in the opening paragraph of *The Power and the Glory* and their conclusion that 'he wasn't carrion yet') or offhand (like the description of the secretary in the 1935 short story 'Special Duties' who 'moused' into the room and where the unusual verb succinctly conveys her diminutive stature and her apologetic demeanour). The situation of *The Ministry of Fear* (1943) is bizarre more than comic – the hero wins a cake at a charity bazaar that, unbeknownst to him, contains important microfilm – and it is rare that the comic spirit breaks through in his work at this stage. It happens unexpectedly in *The Confidential Agent* (1939) during a scene where the villain with the Kafkaesque name of Mr K is being pursued by the hero Mr D who has a gun and is trailing him in a taxi. For his own protection, Mr K keeps trying to get arrested for being drunk and disorderly. There are only two problems: he keeps forgetting to be disorderly; and a stranger keeps intervening on his behalf, saying the police are persecuting him. Moreover, Dostoevsky-like (this might be Greene's homage to *Crime and Punishment*), a crowd has now gathered, to observe and participate in the fun:

> 'But I am drunk,' Mr K said, suddenly, imploringly, 'I am disorderly.'
> The crowd began to laugh. The policeman turned on Mr K 'Now you've started again,' he said. 'We aren't concerned with you.'
> 'Oh yes, we are,' the stranger said.
> A look of agony crossed the policeman's face. He said to Mr K, 'Now why don't you get quietly into a taxi and go home?'
> 'Yes. Yes. I'll do that,' Mr K said, 'Taxi!'
> The taxi drew up beside Mr K and he grabbed thankfully at the handle, opened the door. D smiled at him and said, 'Step in.'
> 'An' now,' the policeman said, 'for you – whatever your name is.'
> 'My name is Hogpit.'
> 'No more back answer,' the policeman said.

> Mr K backed onto the pavement. He said, 'Not that taxi. I won't take that taxi.'
> 'But my name *is* Hogpit.' Several people laughed. He said angrily, 'It's no funnier than Swinburne.'[8]

The extraordinary humour of this scene – almost like early Hitchcock in its Cockney vitality and adroit crosscutting – is all the more notable because there is nothing remotely like it elsewhere in the novel. Given the circumstances under which the novel was written (outlined in the previous chapter), I am convinced that Greene indulged himself at this point for no other reason than he had no idea where he was going. It is as if it occurred to him on the spur of the moment and he ran with it, got carried away with it – indulging a spirit of spontaneous jocularity that was not to surface again in his novel-writing for another three decades, until *Travels With My Aunt* (1969).

Certainly the comic exuberance of that passage in *The Confidential Agent* would not have struck many readers of his novels as very typical of Greene. *Brighton Rock, The Power and the Glory, The Heart of the Matter* and *The End of the Affair* were the works on which his reputation up to the 1960s primarily rested, and he was associated less with comic artistry than with Catholic *angst*. A different personality comes through in his film criticism, which can be witty and waspish, though, even here, as seen in the chagrin of Twentieth Century Fox over the *Wee Willie Winkie* affair, not everyone got the joke. As he said in another context: 'English humour is often puzzling to Americans...Alas, these English jokes! I must try to avoid them.'[9] Part of Greene's anti-Americanism, I suspect, derived from his feeling that they suffered from what has often been called an 'irony deficiency'. He tended to characterise Americans in his novels as essentially humourless, particularly his Quiet American, whom he christened Pyle because he thought him, as he put it, 'a pain in the bum'.

The comic Graham Greene at this stage also comes through in his writing for the screen more than in his novels, largely because he both recognised and revelled in the fact that the cinema was essentially a popular medium. As he said about *The Third Man*: 'We had no desire to move people's political emotions: we wanted to entertain them, to frighten them, to make them laugh.'[10] For those who accuse the cinema of softening and sentimentalising Greene's vision for the screen, it might be worth remembering that it was Greene who wanted a happy ending for *The Third Man*, an idea vetoed – correctly, as Greene acknowledged – by the director, Carol Reed; and it was Greene who came up with the softened ending of the film of *Brighton Rock*. One might also cite the example of *The Fallen Idol*, Carol Reed's 1948 film which Greene had adapted from his short story 'The Basement Room' of 1935. The original story is a grim tale of unwitting betrayal by a boy of a man whom he has hero-worshipped, a betrayal that will have a traumatic effect on the boy's subsequent adult life: in structure and theme, it seems to foreshadow L.P. Hartley's *The Go-Between*. Although the film has elements of this and is often tense and exciting, the overall conception is much more upbeat, progressing finally to a comedy of non-communication. The turning point is a scene in the police station where the boy is being interrogated and is terrified that he might incriminate his friend. In the story, the boy is questioned by a dour policewoman. In the film, he is approached by a breezy prostitute played by Dora Bryan who, when asked by the police to try and get some information out of the lad, cannot help lapsing into ingrained habits. 'Hello, dearie,' she asks, brightly, 'where do you live?' 'Can't you do it without the smile?' asks the policeman at the desk, wearily. From that point, the whole tone of the film lightens.

Similar is the case with *The Third Man*. Although a powerful tale of post-war corruption and betrayal, it is still at times a comedy of confusion, notably when the writer of cheap westerns, Holly Martins is suddenly whisked away in a taxi and he thinks he may have been kidnapped. 'Have you got orders to kill me?' he demands, but it is worse than that: he has to give a lecture on behalf of the British Council on the topic of the modern novel, and is completely thrown by a question on stream-of-consciousness. (Although Greene professed not to like Hitchcock's film of *The 39 Steps* (1935), it is hard to avoid the conclusion that this scene was much influenced by the moment in the Hitchcock when the hero Richard Hannay, on the run from his pursuers, blunders in to a political meeting, is mistaken for the main speaker, and manages to improvise a rallying call against political complacency.) The villain Harry Lime might have an amoral cynicism that is a convincing legacy from a genocidal war, but even his parting line is a joke: 'After all, it's not that awful – you know what the fellow said . . . In Italy for thirty years under the Borgias they had warfare, terror, murder, bloodshed – but they produced Michelangelo, Leonardo da Vinci and the Renaissance. In Switzerland, they had brotherly love, five hundred years of democracy and peace, and what did that produce...The cuckoo clock. So long, Holly.' Not Graham Greene's line actually, but improvised on the spot by Orson Welles. But it is an inspired piece of improvisation because it is absolutely in the spirit of Greene's screenplay – playful, witty, shocking, worldly wise and sardonic.

The word 'sardonic' has often been used to describe Greene both as a writer and as a man. Korda (1980) suggested that the reason that his father, the great film producer and tycoon, Sir Alexander Korda got on so well with Greene was because 'they both had a sardonic temperament'.[11] The Oxford English Dictionary defines 'sardonic' as 'grimly jocular'. As one might expect, the narrator Marlow in Conrad's *Heart of Darkness* expresses the sardonic outlook to perfection when he remarks at one stage: 'Droll thing life is – that mysterious arrangement of merciless logic for a futile purpose.'[12] What is striking there is the contrast between the content and the tone: life as 'mysterious, merciless, futile' but how 'droll'. It is the narrator's drollery that holds the horror of that knowledge at arm's length. Greene's sardonic temperament similarly kept what he defined as the 'panic-fear' of the human condition at a distance, under control, but (like the fearful fiend that stalks the *Ancient Mariner*) also in constant view or awareness. One of the etymological derivations of 'sardonic' refers to the ancient belief that eating a Sardinian plant could result in convulsive laughter ending in death. Two of Greene's most complex heroes – Querry in *A Burnt-Out Case* and Dr Plarr in *The Honorary Consul* – die laughing, or with a laugh on their lips. Laughter can be dangerous in Greene: it can get you killed. But it may also be necessary to keep the horror of life at bay.

One of the most dangerous forms of humour is the practical joke, the danger being one of crossing the boundary into tastelessness and that the person on whom the joke is being played might not find it funny. Greene was an inveterate practical joker. One of his most elaborate was his pretence at founding an entirely imaginary Anglo-Texan club, a joke which he took to extraordinary lengths, in order to sustain the illusion. (Maybe the last laugh was on him: a vast collection of his papers was to be kept in Austin in Texas.) His appearance in the film *Day for Night*, as previously indicated, was essentially a practical joke on the director Francois Truffaut, just as his billing on the credits as 'Henry Graham' (his own first two names) was a practical joke on the audience and critics: in America, Pauline Kael was one of the few who saw through it. In an address to the Graham Greene Festival at Berkhamsted in September 2000, Michael Meyer recalled the occasion when, miffed at not being invited to a party at Cyril Connolly's, Greene telephoned the host in the middle of the evening pretending to be a chimney sweep and saying he was coming to sweep the chimney first thing in the morning: would Connolly therefore ensure that all the furniture was protected with dust covers? Meyer also recalled a long-running saga when Greene rang a retired solicitor listed in the phone book as Graham Greene and, pretending to mistake him for the novelist, proceeded to harangue him for writing pornographic novels. This 'joke' was repeated on several occasions using different voices, resulting in the victim's eventually choosing to go ex-directory. The practical joker is a particular species of comedian. It is a form of comedy with a sadistic edge that gives more pleasure to the person who practises it than to the person on the receiving end. The joke becomes an exercise in power where one can talk of joker and victim, and the comedy becomes a form of embarrassment, humiliation and even torture.[13] Practical jokes have their dark side and are very revealing about the joker. In the BBC's 1993 *Arena* documentary on Greene, Vivien Greene said that 'people think of it as high spirits but I don't think it is . . . I have a theory, and I'm convinced that I'm right, that people who are great on practical jokes are very unhappy . . . ' That would apply to Greene. It was almost like his penchant for travelling[14]: the practical joke was a refuge from boredom. Both in his life and in his writing, it took on a number of varied manifestations.

For example, the hero of Greene's comedy play, *The Complaisant Lover* (1959) is a serial practical joker who likes doing things such as putting musical boxes under chair cushions and watching the embarrassed response.[15] A sense of humour, he says, is an essential ingredient of a successful marriage. That rather depends on whether you see or appreciate the joke and, to some degree, the laugh is on him, for his wife is having an affair with one of the party guests on whom he is playing his jokes. Nevertheless, as Harold Pinter was observing at that time when writing about *The Caretaker*, everything can be made to seem funny, but the point of interest for the dramatist is very often the point at which it becomes *no longer* funny. Greene will poke fun at his hero, particularly because he is a dentist, which, to judge from his writings, seems to have been Greene's least favourite profession.[16] But he does not trivialise his distress when the man finds out the truth and is taken to the point of near-suicide. Indeed, the husband even upstages the lover by the end with a 'practical' proposal for the managing of this love triangle which leaves the lover impaled, as it were, on the comic pun in the title – not 'complacent' as in 'smugly self-satisfied' but 'complaisant' as in 'politely deferential'.

Reviewing the play at the time, Kenneth Tynan had found the characters completely unbelievable, 'partly because John Gielgud's antiseptic direction failed to convince me that the lovers had achieved any significant carnal contact, perhaps because Ralph Richardson performed in a vein of fantasy that seemed incompatible with dentistry'.[17] Curiously, though, while admitting that this does not necessarily add up to dramatic credibility, one cannot help noticing a vein of autobiographical subtext in the material. A practical joker as hero would have an obvious personal reference, and indeed Greene is to give the practical joker divine status in *The Comedians*.[18] Equally personal, though, is the *ménage à trois* proposed by the dry cuckolded husband to the bookish lover of his wife: that has a certain uncomfortable reference to the set-up involving Greene, Catherine Walston and her husband Henry. There is an even more controversial, if oblique, personal reference at another point in the play. At his lowest point, the husband attempts suicide through carbon monoxide poisoning in his garage. Greene's lover at this time, the Swedish actress Anita Bjork, who is probably best known for her superb performance in the title role of Alf Sjoberg's film of *Miss Julie* (1951), had previously been married to the writer Stig Dagerman who in 1953, after eighteen months of marriage, had been found dead in his garage in precisely the circumstances reproduced in the play. A tactless coincidence? It is not an unusual dramatic contrivance : there is a scene in Billy Wilder's romantic comedy, *Sabrina* (1954) that stages a suicide attempt in this manner. Nonetheless, there was some disquiet to say the least at what was thought to be Greene's tastelessness in including such a scene – Anita Bjork never commented – and it has even been suggested that the withholding of the Nobel Prize for Literature from Greene was in some way connected with the residual bitterness accruing from this event.[19]

It may have had something to do with his mood, but Greene's comedy at this time was, as it were, sailing close to the wind. In terms of narrative, his most elaborate practical joke is *Our Man in*

Havana (1958), his satire – even revenge – on the operations of the British Secret Service he knew so well. A vacuum cleaner salesman in Havana, Wormold, has been recruited as a secret agent by the Government's man, Hawthorne. The hero's ignoble name, plus the very locale of his recruitment – the lavatory – are not auspicious auguries. Quite unable to recruit any agents, as he is required to do, Wormold takes the advice of his friend, Dr Hasselbacher – he has outlined his dilemma but in very obscure terms – and decides to invent some. Quite without the capacity to recognise, locate or steal any valuable security documents, he makes them up – sketching the inside of his vacuum cleaners and then passing off these drawings as sketches of mysterious machinery being transported to secret hideaways in Cuba. Back at headquarters in London, the finest security minds of the nation ponder these startling drawings. Hawthorne has a shiver of apprehension when it is suggested to him that they resemble the inside of a giant vacuum cleaner, but is reassured when Wormold tells him his life is in danger: this seems to imply that the agent is telling the truth. Indeed, an attempt is made on Wormold's life at a trade convention but the plan goes wrong and a dog is poisoned. 'The dog it was that died,' remarks Wormold, absently quoting a line from Oliver Goldsmith's comic poem, 'An Elegy on the Death of a Mad Dog', where a man is bitten by a mad dog and is expected to die, but, to everyone's wonderment:

> The man recovered of the bite,
> The dog it was that died.[20]

What is it about mad dogs and Englishmen? Anyway, Wormold is finally rumbled, but what to do with him? He cannot be charged under the Official Secrets Act, because, as he points out, he had invented secrets, he had not given any away. It ends in a typically British rebuke/compromise: a Lectureship and an OBE.

Yet, if *Our Man in Havana* is funny, there is a point at which it becomes no longer funny. Wormold has invented a few agents but then people with the same name start getting killed. He has invented too well, as his friend Dr Hasselbacher tells him; and, for a moment, it seems, we have the outline of an allegory of artistic creativity – the artist invents and then finds his characters taking on a life and death of their own. But this inventiveness is to lead to his friend's death and to Wormold himself becoming a killer. When Wormold is beginning to suspect that things are getting out of control, there is a particularly striking image:

> Until now the mistake had seemed to Wormold fairly simple to deal with. But now it was though he had tugged a stray piece of cotton and a whole suit had begun to unwind.[21]

There is an image in Hitchcock's *Saboteur* (1942) that is rather similar to that but the image it unmistakably evokes for me is Alec Guinness in that great Ealing comedy, *The Man in the White Suit* (1951), directed by Alexander Mackendrick. Guinness plays a scientist who has invented a white suit that never wears out, causing consternation to both management and labour: but, at a point when he is about to be set upon by an angry mob, somebody pulls at his suit and it starts to unravel and disintegrate. In one sense, *Our Man in Havana* is a very Ealingesque conception, and was published in the year Ealing ceased film production: it pits the little individual against the big institution, in the course of which the big institution is made to look cumbersome, pompous and foolish. What distinguishes Mackendrick's Ealing comedies from the norm is that, as in Greene, there is always an undertone of cruelty and complexity to the comedy that undercuts the ostensible cosiness. This is true of *Man in the White Suit* and *Whisky Galore* (1949), and particularly true of Mackendrick's last Ealing comedy, *The Ladykillers* (1955). This film will end on a series of deaths and murders precipitated by an old lady who is an innocent but whose innocence, as is also so often the case in Greene, is lethal – think of Wormold, or Pyle in *The Quiet American*, or the boy in *The Fallen Idol*, or Marie in *A Burnt-Out Case*. ('God preserve us all from innocence,' says Querry in that novel. 'At least the guilty know what they're about.') It is possible that *Our Man in Havana* was influenced by Ealing comedy, as Greene had worked with Ealing personnel before.[22] Indeed, when Greene refused to let Alfred Hitchcock do the movie,[23] it is a pity that the direction was not entrusted to Alexander Mackendrick rather than Carol Reed, who was not quite right for it, lacking the requisite cutting edge of comic cruelty. One of the problems of the film was a fundamental disagreement between Reed and Guinness over how the part of Wormold should be played: Reed wanted him essentially as a cipher and catalyst who basically facilitates the plot whereas Guinness wanted to make him much more of a character. Mackendrick might have been more in sympathy with Guinness's view: he had directed him brilliantly in *White Suit* and *Ladykillers*. In any event, when Guinness was criticised for the dullness of his performance, Greene (in an unpublished letter to Dilys Powell, for example) leapt to his defence, saying the actor was not at fault but 'was utterly unable to play his role with the awful young woman – that is, Jo Morrow – who played the daughter...she was quite intolerable'. As Michael Redgrave observed when playing opposite Audie Murphy in *The Quiet American*: it's one thing getting a performance out of a non-actor, but it's quite another *giving* one opposite someone like that.

If *Our Man in Havana* is a comedy that moves into darker territory, Greene's next novel, *A Burnt-Out Case* is a bleak and deeply serious work that unexpectedly ends in farce – the work in which Greene said he 'discovered Comedy'. Although he discouraged any overt biographical readings of his literary work, there seems no doubt that this novel was as consciously self-revealing as any that Greene ever wrote. It came at a time in his life when he was in deepest despair. His emotional life was in a mess; he felt creatively at a dead end. He abandoned the idea of a novel about a school because living mentally in such surroundings for the next few years would be less preferable than some time in a leper colony in the Congo, so, he said, 'I went to Yonda in search of a burnt-out case.'[24] But it was clearly an extremely stressful and even masochistic, experience. He was to tell Marie-Francois Allain that: 'I lived with a neurotic, Querry, and his presence affected me in the smallest of humdrum details – a little as though an actor playing the part of Othello suddenly realised that he was behaving like Othello in his private life.' (Greene might have been thinking there of the famous 1947 George Cukor film, *A Double Life*, in which an Oscar-winning Ronald Colman plays an actor who does precisely that.) Greene went on: 'The bond between the character and the self is so strong, it can have some disastrous effects on one's own life.'[25] Two other points might be noted here. Greene finally takes the image of leprosy to its literal conclusion in this novel: elsewhere it has been merely a suggestive metaphor, in works such as *Lord Rochester's Monkey* (1974), *England Made Me*, *The Heart of the Matter*, *The End of the Affair* and *The Quiet American*.[26] Also it does seem as if Greene seriously thought that this might be his last novel. 'I had assumed

after *A Burnt-Out Case,*' he wrote, 'that my writing days were finished –
at any rate as far as the novel was concerned.'[27]

A famous Catholic architect, Querry, who has retired from the
human race, who is literally at the end of the road, seeks refuge at a leper
colony in the Congo, where he feels he is beyond human or emotional
reach. No such luck: he is befriended by a man, Rycker and sought
out by a journalist, Parkinson, who spreads news of Querry's where-
abouts. Querry is in despair and, at one stage of the novel, tells a story
to Rycker's wife, Marie, that is clearly an allegory of himself:

> I have told you about my hero's first discovery. His second came
> much later when he realised he was not born to be an artist at all:
> only a very clever jeweller. He made one gold jewel in the shape
> of an ostrich egg:... Everyone said he was a master-technician,
> but he was highly praised too for the seriousness of his subject-
> matter... Suddenly our hero realized how bored he was – he never
> wanted to turn his hand any more to mounting any jewel at all.
> He was finished with his profession – he had come to an end of
> it... However, the fact that his jewels ceased to be popular with
> people in general only made him more popular with the connoisseurs
> who distrust popular success. They began to write books about his
> art... the books all said much the same thing, and when our hero
> had read one, he had read them all.[28]

Marie says: 'Why do you keep on calling him a jeweller, you know
very well he was an architect.' We know very well that he is a novelist.
Greene is essentially talking about himself and in a tone of world-
weariness and self-pity that seems extreme even by his standards.
The mixture of self-justification and self-hatred reminds one of
works like Alexander Pope's *Epistle to Dr Arbuthnot* or Woody Allen's
film, *Stardust Memories* (1980), where the artist-hero lashes out at
friends as well as enemies, admirers as well as critics, as a measure of
his frustration and despair. Querry is to call it a 'disgust of praise –
how it nauseates by its stupidity'.[29] For Greene this came with the
success of *The Heart of the Matter* – in allegorical terms, the gold jewel
in the shape of the ostrich egg in Querry's story – and then *The End
of the Affair*, which attracted a huge volume of letters to him from
what he called 'the victims of religion', asking him for spiritual and
theological advice and solace that he felt ill-equipped to provide. Out

of this feeling of exhaustion and exploitation, which Greene likened to being like a man without medical knowledge in a village stricken with plague, the character of Querry was conceived. He was a man, like Greene, for whom success had proved even more dangerous and disorientating than failure.

And then something quite extraordinary happens. In the midst of this deeply personal and superbly crafted study of spiritual despondency and of the creative man at the end of his tether, comedy rears its head. In the first chapter of the novel, it has been said of Querry that 'he wondered when it was that he had first begun to detest laughter like a bad smell'.[30] Yet in the leper colony, Querry slowly begins to unwind and relax a little, the novel building to a startling moment for Dr Colin, who runs the colony, when Querry cracks a joke. 'An unexpected sound made the doctor look up; Querry's face was twisted into the rictus of a laugh. The doctor realised with astonishment that Querry had perpetrated a joke.'[31] The word 'perpetrated' is beautifully chosen there: its very elaborateness suggests *real* effort.

Everything will now begin to build to a climax where tragedy teeters on farce. Rycker mistakenly believes that Querry has had an affair with his wife, Marie and made her pregnant (he knows of Querry's terrible reputation with women in the past). It is not true, but Marie, who has fallen in love with Querry, has told her husband that this is indeed the case. 'Her smile of sad and fallen trust,' thinks Querry when she tells him of this, 'was worthy of Bernhardt's Marguerite Gauthier on her deathbed'.[32] The theatrical imagery begins to intensify. Rycker turns up at Father Thomas's in a rage and holding a gun: 'Rycker made for the door. He stood there for a moment as though he were on stage and had forgotten his exit line.'[33] When he has gone, Father Jean likens the scene to those Palais Royal farces he has read and ventures the opinion that: 'Sometimes I think God was not entirely serious when he gave man the sexual instinct.'[34] Another of His practical jokes, perhaps. (The eponymous hero of Greene's late masterpiece, *Monsignor Quixote* will have a similar intuition when he inadvertently attends a pornographic movie: far from being shocked, he has to stop himself from falling about laughing.) Meanwhile, Rycker, who has the same name as the villain in the classic Western, *Shane* (1953), is behaving like a gun-slinger and is clearly intent on a showdown.[35] 'That this should happen to me,' says Querry. 'The innocent adulterer. That's not a bad title for a comedy.' He goes out to try and pacify Rycker but is shot: 'Querry made an odd awkward sound which the doctor by now had learned to interpret as a laugh, and Rycker fired twice.' 'He shouldn't have laughed,' Rycker cries, but Querry was not laughing at him, only at himself. 'He doesn't laugh easily,' the doctor explains, and Querry's dying words are: 'Absurd, this is absurd, or else...'[36] To borrow a phrase from Alfred Kazin, it is as if the age of anxiety has imperceptibly slipped into the age of absurdity.

It is a wonderful scene in its balance between tension and slapstick, and I do think it represents a significant stylistic and philosophical shift in Greene's work. From *A Burnt-Out Case* onwards, the themes will remain much the same – faith, fidelity and betrayal, political oppression and sympathy for the underdog – but the style will be more varied, the outlook more generous. That this coincides with an upturn in his life does not seem coincidental, and is a view shared by his publisher, Max Reinhardt who noted that, after Greene's meeting with Yvonne Cloetta towards the end of his writing of *A Burnt-Out Case*, his work 'was a little more outward and more cheerful. Of course, the relationship with Yvonne Cloetta benefited Graham as a writer'.[37] In the short story 'Under the Garden' from the 1963 collection of short stories, *A Sense of Reality*, the narrator will say at one stage that 'it was as if...the only important things in life were two, laughter and fear'.[38] By 'laughter', Greene explained, he meant the 'importance of a certain sense of fun'.[39]

Admittedly, his next novel, *The Comedians* (1966) will be a ferocious evocation of the brutality of political dictatorship in Haiti, as if he were responding in part to the criticism of *Our Man in Havana* that he had been a little too frivolous about political oppression in Cuba under Batista. But even here, there is an ironic tone. The main characters have the bland names of Brown, Smith and Jones, partly, Greene argued, because it is one way to avoid libel actions, but also, one feels, as a strategy of depersonalisation: it is as if we have all become one of Harry Lime's little dots (as he looks down, in all senses, at humanity from the Great Wheel) and are playing indistinguishable insignificant roles in the Human Comedy. Brown is a fairly sober-faced narrator, but the Smiths, for once in Greene, are likeable Americans who believe world aggression can be accounted for by too much acidity in the stomach and are on a mission to convert Haiti to vegetarianism. Jones is a complete charlatan involved in a dubious deal with the government that falls through and necessitates his disguise in drag at one stage, but he does make people laugh and dies a heroic death. Cosmically, the novel seems to be suggesting, rather like Eliot's Prufrock, that we are not Hamlets in this life, but more like Rosencrantz and Guidenstern – comic figures on the outside of the action, just wondering what is going on. In a travel article about Papa Doc's Haiti called 'Nightmare Republic' published in *The Sunday Telegraph* (September 1963) prior to the writing of *The Comedians*, Greene wrote about the people 'living in a reign of terror which has often about it the atmosphere of a farce. The irresponsible is in control. The banana skin is a deadly one, but it remains a banana skin'. That is part of the atmosphere he wanted to get across in the novel, and it echoes something that the lover in *The Complaisant Lover* has said in Act One Scene Two: 'We aren't allowed a tragedy nowadays without a banana skin to slip on and make it funny. But it hurts just the same.' That is the other dimension of the banana skin that he wanted to get into *The Comedians*: that it hurts just the same.

In the late 1960s, Greene published two of his most overtly comic works. His collection of short stories, *May We Borrow Your Husband?* (1967) was written, he said, ' in a single mood of sad hilarity'.[40] In the novel, *Travels With My Aunt* (1969), Greene, in his words, 'attempted to treat humorously a serious theme, old age and death'.[41] I suspect he was much influenced in this by another comic novel about death, *Memento Mori* (1959) by a Catholic novelist, Muriel Spark, whom he both admired and supported. Even critics generally sympathetic to Greene have had their problems with *Travels With My Aunt* – he even gently has to chide one of his most devoted followers, Father Leopoldo Duran for underrating it – and some find it diffuse, uncharacteristic and self-indulgent. Yet there is no other novel of Greene that conveys so much enjoyment in the writing, and it is no accident that it is dedicated, and in a comic way, to Yvonne Cloetta, who had had such a transforming effect on his life.[42] The humour of the novel is deliciously varied. It emerges in quirky detail (an African valet improbably called Wordsworth, pot being smuggled amongst a mother's ashes), cheeky anecdote (one about premature cremation, another about a Church for dogs that seems both an homage to, and worthy of, Evelyn Waugh), and sly in-jokes (a character called Visconti after the villain of Greene's favourite childhood book, *The Viper of Milan*, or flowers that the hero grows being called 'Ben-Hurs', a recollection of the epic on which Greene had been invited to do some rewriting on account of the anticlimax after the Crucifixion). There is any amount of farcical incident, culminating in the hero's being arrested in Paraguay for blowing his nose. Towering above all this is the central character of Aunt Augusta, who attacks everything with gusto (hence her name?) and whose logic is unassailable even though it never quite veers into conventional sense (e.g. how can she have planned anything illegal, she argues when arrested for smuggling, when she has never read any of the laws and has no idea what they are?). Behind all this frivolity, nevertheless, are two themes that Greene took seriously and treats sensitively. The first has to do with the situation of a staid, repressed hero, Henry Pulling, who suddenly has a glimpse of an exciting anarchic alternative world (Aunt Augusta's) which frightens and attracts him at the same time: will he embrace it or recoil from it? It is an intriguing variation on the Holly Martins/ Harry Lime relationship in *The Third Man*. Also a theme of the novel – which is: live life to the full, it is the only one you have – is something Greene would have recognised as a key theme in one of the writers he most revered, Henry James, particularly in a novel such as *The Ambassadors*. It is a comedy about death but also about the saving of someone from a living death.

If Greene makes light of political oppression in Paraguay in *Travels With My Aunt*, he will make amends through a serious treatment of the theme in a later novel, *The Honorary Consul*. It is striking how works of Greene can often be paired in this way. The Batista regime is let off lightly in *Our Man in Havana*, so Greene compensates by a savage exposure of a similarly despotic regime in *The Comedians*. He makes comedy out of adultery in *The Complaisant Lover* but the same theme leads to religious transcendence in *The End of the Affair*. British Intelligence is satirised as incompetent in *Our Man in Havana* but criticised for its ruthlessness in *The Human Factor*: even the murder of a dog in the former, which is treated comically, is paralleled by the murder of a dog in the latter, which is deadly serious. It is not simply that he is balancing comedy with seriousness, entertainment with profundity: the implication behind the strategy seems to be that *every* story has at least two sides and could be told tragically or comically. Every situation has its inverse reflection – Greene will demonstrate that in one of his most serious plays, *The Living Room* as well as in one of his most light-hearted sketches, the Pinter pastiche, *Yes and No* (1983).

There is a particularly telling epigraph to *The Honorary Consul* where Greene quotes Thomas Hardy:

> All things merge in one another – good into evil,
> generosity into justice, religion into politics.

And one might add: tragedy into comedy. 'The World is a comedy to those who think, a tragedy to those that feel', wrote Horace Walpole. As most of us do a bit of both at some time or another, whichever predominates is always in a state of flux.

Perhaps this is true of character too: every character has his or her double. Querry certainly feels this about Parkinson in *A Burnt-Out Case*: 'You are my looking-glass. I can talk to a looking-glass, but one can be a little afraid of one too.'[43] As I have argued, there is a similar dimension to the Holly Martins/Harry Lime relationship. At the end of *Ways of Escape*, Greene reveals that he has become aware of a Double stalking his footsteps and for whom he is often being mistaken. To his surprise, the Other often appears in journalistic stories about 'the writer being blackmailed, or being imprisoned in India, or holidaying in Geneva'. The BBC made an amusing and inventive documentary on this theme, and it is almost as if Greene's own pranks on his identity (the joke on Francois Truffaut, the harrying of the retired solicitor with the same name) are coming back to haunt him. Who is this Other? Is this Other the real Graham Greene and the writer the impostor? 'I found myself shaken by a metaphysical doubt,' remarks Greene at the end of this second volume of memoirs. 'Had I been the impostor all the time? Was I the Other?'[44] It is interesting that 'metaphysical doubt' at that stage of Greene's life was a source of wry humour rather than spiritual anxiety. It is also interesting that the story Greene relates is so similar to the plot of Alfred Hitchcock's *North by Northwest* (1959), the film Hitchcock went on to make when Greene had refused him the rights to *Our Man in Havana*. Hitchcock's plot also concerns a hero (Cary Grant) mistaken for another, who finds it impossible to prove his own identity to his pursuers despite the fact that the man he is supposed to be does not exist, and who finally takes on the identity of this non-being.

I want to press the connection between Greene and *North by Northwest* a little further. Up to *A Burnt-Out Case*, if I were looking for a statement or epigraph that might encapsulate Greene's world view,

I would have been drawn to that Conrad aphorism from *Heart of Darkness* quoted earlier: the sardonic tone ('droll thing life is') and the bleak vision ('that mysterious arrangement of merciless logic for a futile purpose') seemed to define the outlook of Greene's work, and indeed the point he had come to by that time in his life. Even Conrad's punctuation seemed eloquent: the dash coming after the tone and before the statement seems like the narrator's outstretched arm keeping the horror of that knowledge at arm's length. But after *A Burnt-Out Case*, I believe Greene grew away from that darkness although never entirely losing sight of it. He mellowed; the comic spirit came increasingly to his aid. It is in that context that *North by Northwest* becomes pertinent and a different epigraph comes to mind. It is the moment when a CIA man has just heard about Cary Grant's plight: that he has been mistaken for a non-existent agent; that he has been forced to guzzle bourbon in an endeavour to make him crash his car; that he is thought to have stabbed an ambassador in the back, and has last been seen running for his life from the United Nations building in New York. 'Brother...' says the CIA man. 'It's so horribly sad, why is it I feel like laughing?'

That is surely the atmosphere of the ending of *A Burnt-Out Case*. It is horribly sad – this ridiculous misunderstanding which is creating such hatred and unhappiness – but why is it you feel like laughing? Fatally, Querry cannot restrain his laughter at the absurdity of it all and it costs him his life. But, for Greene, the laughter of Querry – for the purposes of this novel, a character who is indisputably Greene's Other – comes, I would argue, as a form of deliverance. He thought *A Burnt-Out Case* was to be his *Heart of Darkness*. Instead, thanks to the comedy, it turned out – unexpectedly, almost miraculously (and uncannily recalling the very last shot of *North by Northwest*) – the light at the end of the tunnel.

6
A Sort of Autobiography: Epigraphs and Dedications

An author's work changes, as his ideas change, with the years, and the epigraphs he uses, like his books, form a sort of autobiography, beginning with the innocent disclosures of immaturity and ending with the uncertainties and fears of old age.

– Graham Greene[1]

Most of what he [Greene] said about himself was a cover story.

– John Le Carré[2]

I grew clever at evasion.

– Graham Greene[3]

In the opening chapter of *The Human Factor*, it is said of the British Secret Service hero, Castle (who is later to be revealed as a double agent) that: 'except on really important occasions, he always preferred the truth. The truth can be double-checked'. Truth as strategic policy as much as personal principle: what you disclose is limited to what can be checked. One feels there is a lot of Greene in that. From childhood, particularly in his having to negotiate divided loyalties between his headmaster father and his school friends on the opposite border, so to speak, secrecy and evasion became second nature to him. His fiction would slide into disguised autobiography just as his autobiographies occlude the whole truth, not so much by inclusion as by omission. *A Sort of Life* and *Ways of Escape* tell us next to nothing about, for example, his parents, his marriage, his affairs and his children. But what a great title *A Sort of Life* is (and Greene was always good at titles). As he explains, it is a description of the limitations of autobiography as a form (it can only tell a partial truth); it is also an evocation of a life only partially fulfilled, like most people's (it calls to mind Stan Barstow's evocative title, *A Kind of Loving*, for the sad and compromised relationship at the novel's core); it implies the idea of autobiography as a kind of 'sorting' – sorting through one's memories, sorting out one's priorities; and it conveys the implication that one might not be getting the whole story. Like Alfred Hitchcock, who took some trouble over the creation of a persona and reputation that projected an image of himself that he endorsed, Greene tended to disclose only those sides of himself that contributed to the Greene mythology. For the rest of the time he left clues.

How much does Greene's fiction reveal about his life and personality, and vice-versa? This might sound something of an old-fashioned question, particularly in the light of the now dated but massively influential article by W.K. Wimsatt and M.C. Beardsley, 'The Intentional Fallacy' (published in *The Theory of Literary Criticism*) which argued that the author's supposed intention was not relevant to the literary critic, who can only trust the words on the page. In a very interesting recent counter to that argument in relation, particularly, to Greene's *The Power and the Glory*,[4] Kenneth R. Morefield refers to Gerard Genette's categories of 'epitexts and paratexts', which, he explains, is a theory that moderates the absolutism of the Wimsatt/Beardsley position, and are interpretations, comments and elements, 'not materially appended to the text within the same volume', that 'mediate' the story being told. In the case of Greene, these could be letters about the text, essays that reflect on them, those parts of his autobiographies where he talks about the writing of them and what he adjudges to be their successes and failures, all of which contribute to a sense of what the author had in mind and what the texts are meant to mean. Morefield uses Greene's extra-textual data most deftly to argue for his particular interpretation of *The Power and the Glory*. In this chapter, I want to take this a little further and show how Greene has left quite conscious clues about his self and his work in what one might call the spaces between the primary textual matter. I am thinking of the veritable network of clues, implications and autobiographical hints that are contained in the epigraphs and dedications, not to mention the signifying importance of titles and characters' names. These too constitute a sort of life.

Greene himself thought that the best clues to the deeper meanings of his works lay in his carefully chosen epigraphs, which he collected and published in a separate volume called *Why The Epigraph?* (1989). In one sense, the epigraphs underline his literary aspiration and display his literary erudition. The range of reference is extraordinary: from Sir Thomas Browne to Cardinal Newman, from Dryden to George Herbert, from Dante to Auden, from Hardy to Melville, from Péguy to Flaubert. The only frivolity he allows himself – though it is very apposite – is a quotation from Walt Disney's Goofy ('All the world owes me a living') as the epigraph for *England Made Me*. For one of his suppressed novels, *Rumour at Nightfall*, he has an epigraph from Thomas Traherne, and he observes: 'I am sure this epigraph described my intention, ... but I have never re-read it (i.e. the novel) and I have quite forgotten what my intention was.'[5] 'Why The Epigraph?' becomes almost as teasing a question in the Greene mystery as *Why Do I Write?* In the introduction to the volume, Greene suggests playfully that the epigraph is one way of dealing with the perennial journalistic question, 'What is your new novel about?' – by which they mean 'plot'. But, as Greene says, the plots are never what his novels are 'about': it was the epigraph that suggested the theme. This implies that, for Greene, choosing the right epigraph was very important, because it crystallised in his mind the novel's core idea and also guided him in terms of style and content. Moreover, as noted in the first epigraph of this chapter, he believes they are not only about an individual book but cumulatively revealing about the author. As he notes at the end of his introduction, the epigraph he would claim for his entire output would be Browning's 'Our interest's on the dangerous edge of things...' from *Bishop Blougram's Apology*, where Browning's Bishop is talking to his inter-locutor, Mr Gigadibs. 'Mr Gigadibs to me,' says Greene, 'represents all those reviewers who think the novel consists of a plot'.[6] So, not only did the epigrams help him find a focus for his work, they were obliquely revealing about him, Greene as always preferring to reveal himself by stealth and implication more than direct disclosure. After all, why is that quotation from Browning so important to Greene? Why was he so interested in the dangerous edge?

The epigraphs can be grouped under different categories. Some texts have no epigraphs, like *The Third Man* and *The Tenth Man* (1985), because, as Greene explains, they were written to be filmed rather than read. His prologue to his play, *Carving A Statue* (1964) is more an epitaph than an epigraph, bewailing the anguish of composition, the torture of performance, and the clash of conception between author and leading actor (Ralph Richardson), who, said Greene, believed he was playing Ibsen.[7] A number explicitly locate the core of the novels' themes as they actually provide the title for the text. This is true of *The Man Within* (Sir Thomas Browne), *It's A Battlefield* (Kinglake), *The Lawless Roads* (Edwin Muir) and *The Captain and the Enemy* (George Birmingham). It is also true of his volume of verse, *Babbling April*, which is taken from a poem by Edna St Vincent Millay ('It's not enough that yearly, down this hill / April / Comes like an idiot, babbling and strewing flowers'). Titles were always very important to Greene: he claimed to have sold *The Ministry of Fear* to a film company on the basis of the title alone, even though it is actually taken from Wordsworth's *Prelude*[8]; and Bryan Forbes tells the story that when Greene's American publisher objected to the title of *Travels With My Aunt*, Greene's breezy riposte was to suggest that it was easier to change publisher than to change title.[9] Other epigraphs seem to be especially eloquent on the theme and the mood of the text. The Dryden epigraph for *The Power and the Glory*, for example ('The inclosure narrow'd; the sagacious power / Of hounds and death drew nearer every hour'), conjures up in a single couplet the entire atmosphere of the novel: of time and space running out; of increasing claustrophobia; of the situation of being hounded unto death; and a wonderfully ambiguous phrase like 'sagacious power' touching on many areas, both political and religious, in the novel. The two quotations that head *The Quiet American* seem deliberately paired to evoke the personalities of the two main characters: a quotation from A.H. Clough ('I do not like being moved . . .') that seems to express Fowler's distaste for involvement, his dispassionate nature; and one from Byron ('This is the patent age of new inventions / For killing bodies and for saving souls / All propagated with the best intentions') that could scarcely better express Greene's disquiet at America's pious and naive foreign policy interventionism, as embodied in the character of Pyle.

There are epigraphs that precede two particular works of Greene that seem to go further than an expression of the core theme of the text and instead get to the heart of Greene's mood when he was writing them. Take this, for instance: 'Man has places in his heart which do not yet exist, and into them enters Suffering in order that they may have existence' (Leon Bloy). That is the prelude, as it were, to *The End of the Affair*: it seems to me not only an expression of Bendrix's suffering in the novel, but also of Greene's, his heart opened up and exposed and tormented in a manner he had not deemed possible until his affair with Catherine Walston. The capitalisation of 'Suffering' is especially telling. The expression of a deeply personal pain expressed in the epigraphs reaches its climax, I believe, in *A Burnt-Out Case*. There is a quotation from Dante which is translated as: 'I did not die; yet nothing of life remained,' which surely corresponds to Greene's feelings of world-weariness at the time. The other epigraph is from a pamphlet on leprosy by R.V. Wardeker and it is worth quoting in its entirety:

Within limits of normality, every individual loves himself. In cases where he has a deformity or abnormality or develops it later, his own aesthetic sense revolts and he develops a sort of disgust towards himself. Though, with time, he becomes reconciled to his deformities, it is only at the conscious level. His sub-conscious mind, which continues to bear the mark of injury, brings about certain changes in his whole personality, making him suspicious of society.

That seems to me more than a comment on the leper or even on the central character, Querry: it is nothing short of an expression of the tormented state of mind of the author as he embarked on that novel, alluding to his self-disgust, his social alienation and a perceived psychological, rather than physical, deformity in his own personality.

Equally revealing, however, in autobiographical terms, are the dedications. As is fitting, a number of them are to members of his own family. *A Sort of Life* describes his childhood memories as crying 'for rescue [from the unconscious] like the survivors of a shipwreck'[10]; and the book is dedicated 'For the survivors' – that is, his brothers Raymond and Hugh, and his sister, Elisabeth, who share the same background and framework of early experience. (The image of surviving a shipwreck was a powerful one for Greene: he had an enormous fear of the canal near his home in Berkhamsted and recurrent nightmares of death by drowning.) *Doctor Fischer of Geneva* (1980) is dedicated to his daughter Caroline because he had the idea for the novel while spending one Christmas at her home; and *The Human Factor* is dedicated to his sister, Elisabeth Dennys to whom Greene was devoted and who, as he comments in the dedication, 'cannot deny some responsibility': it was Elizabeth who had recruited him for the Secret Service. Political books, such as *The Quiet American* and *Getting to Know the General* are dedicated to friends who have accommodated him and opened his eyes to the political realities of the country; *The Honorary Consul* is dedicated to his publisher in South America, Victoria Ocampu. Curiously, the dedication in *The Comedians*, Greene's first novel since his move from Heinemann to the Bodley Head, is more literary than political. It is to his long-standing friend and literary colleague, A.S. Frere (who is also cited as dedicatee in *Loser Takes All*) and is in the nature of an apology for failing, despite his best efforts, to ensure Frere's continuation as managing director of Heinemann. Similarly, *Monsignor Quixote* is dedicated to a close friend of his later years, Father Leopoldo Duran, who is part inspiration for the eponymous hero, and to an enduring close friend from his early years, Tom Burns, who, during the war, had become press attaché at the British Embassy in Madrid, encouraging Greene to visit Spain, and who had earlier worked at Longman's and activated the publication of *The Lawless Roads*. For all his reputation as a loner, the dedications do suggest a real capacity for friendship in Greene, and also for gratitude. They suggest too that the dedications were very important to Greene in personal terms as well as in terms of literary inspiration. I cannot think of another major novelist of the century for whom the dedication seemed so important and so resonant. They were another form of indirect revelation, something to be decoded, which might suggest that, although Greene gave you, in John Le Carré's words, 'a cover story' for his life, he was not entirely averse to having that cover blown.

Perhaps the most striking aspect of the dedications is the romantic subtext they imply, that is sometimes quite removed from the ostensible subjects of the texts. One of the most astute of all critics on Greene, Judith Adamson, has noted that quite a lot of the dedications are to women. She links that to Greene's confession to Marie-Francois Allain that he was 'a bad husband and a fickle lover'. 'Were these dedications apologies to them?' she asks. 'Do these books contain hidden explanations of what went wrong or, in the case of *Travels With My Aunt*, what went right? Or was Graham's apparent inability to create more independently spirited fictional women simply typical of the male writers of his generation, rather than a reflection of the anguish and antagonism that seems to have characterised his relations with women?'[11] The last question is particularly interesting because the five women who assumed especial importance in Greene's personal life after he had separated from his wife – Dorothy Glover, Catherine Walston, Jocelyn Rickards, Anita Bjork and Yvonne Cloetta – tended to be independently minded in a way his fictional heroines were not. 'The women he loved,' said Michael Shelden, 'were neither too possessive nor conventional. They were free-thinking and unintimidated by his fame'.[12]

The dedications pick a trail through the development of Greene's emotional life. The early dedications are to his wife – *The Man Within* ('For Vivien'), *Stamboul Train* ('For Vivien Candace, with all my love'), *England Made Me* ('To Vivien, With Ten Years' Love, 1925–1935'). *Journey Without Maps* has a dedication adorned by a quotation: it reads 'Dedicated To My Wife', which is then followed by a rather pointed quotation from William Plomer, 'I carry you like a passport everywhere.' The image of the passport must have seemed somewhat poignant to Vivien at this time, being increasingly aware of Greene's habitual restlessness: it gives another context for her nickname for her husband at this time as 'Otis B. Driftwood'. But aside from *The Heart of the Matter*, where the dedication is in the form of initials to Greene's wife and children, there are no dedications to Vivien after the mid-1930s, which is one way of signalling, or reading, the beginnings of the breakdown of their relationship. His new relationship with Dorothy Glover is indicated in the dedications, though in a disguised way. A limited first edition of *A Gun for Sale* was inscribed 'For DG with very great love, Graham'[13]; and *The Confidential Agent* was dedicated to Dorothy Craigie, which was her professional name as graphic designer and illustrator of children's books, including those written by Greene. Her intense relationship with Greene remains a somewhat enigmatic affair, as Dorothy herself, who never married, seemed self-effacing in a way not true of his other women. 'That ugly dwarf,' was Catherine Walston's description of her, according to Michael Shelden; and, in her single encounter with her, Vivien could only recall a 'short, stout figure with blue glasses'.[14] Catherine Walston was much more obviously charismatic, and Greene's affair with her during the late 1940s and early 1950s (it actually dragged on longer than that but it was at its most intense there) was emotionally the most traumatic and wrenching affair of his life, partly no doubt because of its scandalous nature, Catherine being married to a prominent English Lord. For the English edition of *The End of the Affair*, which of course is a partial portrait of their relationship, Greene had the discreet dedication: 'For C.'[15] Further from home, and away from people intimately involved in this story, he obviously assumed he could be a bit more open, and the American edition has the dedication: 'For Catherine.' By the time of his play, *The Living Room*, however, in 1953, such discretion has been cast aside, and there is something declamatory and almost desperate in the way the dedication is now not only explicit but capitalised: 'TO CATHERINE WITH LOVE'. Is it the end of the affair? It was to be the last romantic dedication of his work for sixteen years until the appearance of *Travels With My Aunt* in 1969; and the dedication itself, as Greene surely intended, has the happy tone and private allusiveness of the novel itself. 'For H.H.K.,' it reads, 'who helped me more than I can tell'. 'H.H.K.' is not a name but a nickname: 'happy, healthy kitten', which was his pet name for Yvonne Cloetta, whom he had met when in the depths of despair during the period of *A Burnt-Out Case*, and who irradiated the last thirty years of his life. This in turn is reflected in the dedication to *The Captain and the Enemy*. 'For Y,' it reads (the initial protecting her identity?), 'with all the memories we share of nearly thirty years'.

These epigraphs and dedications form a curious appendage to Greene as a writer and seem to me to add something to an understanding of the literature and the biography. It is generally agreed that there was something instinctively secretive and evasive in Greene's personality. He would even liken the very practice of novel-writing to the activity of spying. 'I suppose,' he wrote, 'that every novelist has something in common with a spy; he watches, he overhears, he seeks motives and analyses character and, in his attempt to serve literature, he is unscrupulous.'[16] Although he has denied that his characters are self-revelations (they are certainly never self-justifications) and counselled against a too easy identification between author and hero, it is nevertheless difficult not to see a lot of Greene in, say, the character of Bendrix in *The End of the Affair*, who surely consciously shares a lot of the author's writing habits, or Querry in *A Burnt-Out Case*, who shares the same artistic dilemma and spiritual anguish that Greene experienced at that time. But they are hidden, or modified, by the mantle of literature, which gives Greene his escape route from overt self-exposure. Norman Sherry put this very well when he was characterising the marriage in *The Heart of the Matter* and suggesting how closely it paralleled the marital tensions Greene was experiencing with Vivien: 'Novels declare themselves as fictions not as personal histories, though they mine the personal terrain. Greene always felt that so long as he presented his intimate experiences as fiction, his secrets would remain unrecognised, and this appealed to his guarded nature.'[17] That seems to me both a provocative and precise observation about the relation between fiction and autobiography in Greene's work. But the epigraphs and dedications add another layer to this, it seems to me: they are moments when Greene slightly lowers his guard. As the first epigraph to this chapter discloses, the epigraphs become, as Greene concedes, a form of autobiography. And the dedications become a cumulative record of love, changing partners and publishers, friendship and gratitude, that modify our responses both to the works and to the man. They give another side to a character who, for all his reticence and loner instincts, seems to have inspired and acknowledged exceptional affection. It may be that Judith Adamson is right and that the dedications to the women in his life are a form of apology: he has not managed to create in his fiction a female character to match their complexity and preciousness. It adds to the mystery too. Why would a man with such an apparent taste for privacy leave so many clues to his private life, in the form of dedications whose volume and resonance surpass that of any other modern novelist I can think of? Behind this façade, did Greene have the subconscious wish of every spy, criminal, Catholic and human being: the compulsion to confess?

7
The Green Baize Door

If you pushed open a green baize door in a passage by my father's study, you entered another passage deceptively similar, but none the less you were on alien ground...one was aware of fear and hate.

– The Lawless Roads[1]

There is always one moment in childhood when the door opens and lets the future in.

– The Power and the Glory[2]

Heaven lies about us in our infancy!

– William Wordsworth[3]

Hell lies about us in our infancy.

– Graham Greene[4]

In an essay entitled 'The Burden of Childhood' (1950), Greene wrote: 'There are certain writers, as different as Dickens from Kipling, who never shake off the burden of their childhood...All later experience seems to have been related to these months or years of unhappiness... Dickens learnt sympathy, Kipling cruelty...'[5] One of the features of Greene's criticism is his fascination with different accounts of childhood. It comes through in his admiration for works as diverse as Henry James's *The Turn of the Screw* and the first volume of Herbert Read's autobiography, *The Innocent Eye*. It can be felt in his passionate account of *Oliver Twist*, where, unlike Orwell, Greene seems less moved by the novel's broad social anger than by Dickens's specific rendering of one boy's nightmarish introduction to the world. 'Oliver's predicament,' Greene wrote, 'the nightmare fight between the darkness, where the demons walk, and the sunlight, where ineffective goodness makes its last stand in a condemned world, will remain part of our imagination forever.'[6] It will be remembered from a previous chapter, the enormous impact made on him of the film, *These Three* (1936), William Wyler's film version of Lillian Hellman's play, *The Children's Hour*, which, although softened for the screen, still conveyed the evil and terror of a child's world to chilling effect. 'The audience laughed when the smudged feeble child repeated to her schoolfellow and torturer under threat of betrayal a solemn "knightly" oath of vassalage,' he wrote, 'but it was a terrifying and admirably chosen example of the taboos which exist at that age in that egoistic world, compared with which the adult appears almost kindly and honest.'[7] It is not hard to sense a critic writing feelingly from personal experience there. Almost equally revealing is his review of Wyler's film of the following year, *Dead End* (1937), where the work's social tract on the link between poverty and crime is upstaged by Greene's emphasis on the fascination of the young Dead End kids for the gangster Baby-Face Martin (Humphrey Bogart). 'They carry his baton in their pockets,' Greene writes. 'He was brought up in the same dead end and like a friendly Old Boy he gives them tips – how to catch another gang unaware, how to fling a knife.'[8] The slightly incongruous reference to 'Old Boy' there implies something more about Greene's background than the character's, as if the situation again has a personal resonance. Certainly his admiration for Bogart's performance of the gangster – 'the ruthless sentimentalist who has melodramatized himself from the start' – might well have fed into his characterisation of another baby-faced killer, Pinkie in *Brighton Rock*. In Martin's case, the 'baby-face' is a melancholy reminder that, for all his fine clothes, he is still a Dead End kid at heart; that, like Pinkie, he has never escaped from the doomed aura of his childhood.

Dennis Potter has said that, 'for any writer, the first fourteen years of his or her life are the crucible, no matter what you do'.[9] There is an echo of that in Greene's review of Leon Edel's biography of the early years of Henry James. Talking of the special fascination of the biographer of a writer's early formative years, Greene mentions 'the strange accidents that seem to decide not only that this child shall be a writer, but what kind of a writer this child shall be'.[10] (There could be no better definition for the intention behind this literary biography.) One might think here of semi-autobiographical masterpieces like James Joyce's *A Portrait of the Artist as a Young Man*, D.H. Lawrence's *Sons and Lovers* and Thomas Mann's *Tonio Kröger* as works about childhood that contain the key not only to the writer's subsequent artistry but also to the nature of that artistry. During the review, Greene makes two comments about James that seem to me to have particular applicability to Greene himself. One concerns his discussion of the famous 'mysterious accident' which befell James in his youth while helping to work a pump to put out a fire, and into which all kinds of symbolic and even Freudian meanings have been read. 'I remember many years ago,' writes Greene, 'being taken to task for suggesting that the accident was not, in fact, serious, but that its mystery and importance were deliberately inflated by James to explain his non-participation in the Civil War – in which his younger brothers behaved with exemplary gallantry.'[11] It is tempting to compare that with the 'Russian Roulette' story in Greene's youth, or Hitchcock's incarceration in a police cell, as a young boy, as a practical joke: a tall tale whose precise authenticity is difficult to verify but whose significance is difficult to exaggerate because it seems precisely the moment in those artists' eyes where, in Greene's memorable phrase, the door opens and lets in the future. This intuition might be coupled with another moment in the review when Greene comments on Henry James's autobiographical accounts of his early life: 'he was not a mere bundle of sensibilities, he was a man of great toughness, not unaware of the legend he was creating'.[12] It is hard to think of a sentence more applicable to Greene himself: one can imagine his being aware of this even as he penned it about James. 'Childhood is the bank balance of the writer,' Greene would say,[13] the fund of experiences, impressions, fantasies on which a writer draws for the rest of his life; and the burden of his own childhood – or, more precisely, his own perception and interpretation of it – was to have a profound effect on his writing. As we shall see, one of his finest short stories, 'The Basement Room' (1936) is specifically on that theme.

'Three minutes in a bed or against a wall,' muses the killer, Raven in *A Gun for Sale*, 'and then a lifetime for the one that's born'.[14] Greene's own childhood was hardly as bleak as that, but, from his own account, it had its own morbidities. His first memory was of a dead dog lying at the bottom of his pram; at the age of six, he saw a man commit suicide by cutting his own throat; he had recurrent dreams of death by drowning and claimed to have dreamt of the sinking of the Titanic before it had actually happened. As a child, he was hypersensitive, crying a lot, a trait he carried into his adult life, being particularly sensitive to sentimental films. Blame or praise seemed to be equally painful. 'To be praised was agony,' he wrote, 'I would crawl immediately under the nearest table.'[15] In so far as he described them at all, he pictured his mother and father as rather remote figures who were not given to shows of affection, and something of that may have rubbed off onto Greene's own temperament according to his cousin Barbara, who thought that, with the exception of a few people he was close to, Greene viewed humanity with the clinical detachment of a scientist. Towards the end of her life, Greene's Aunt Eva told Norman Sherry that Graham 'was very different from any other child I have ever known. I just never knew whether he was as a child pleased or unhappy, approved or didn't approve.'[16] This childhood trait of secrecy was to be carried into adulthood. In *A Sort of Life*, Greene writes a lot about his childhood phobias, which he listed as drowning, blood, moths, birds, bats and sports. His favourite game was playing hide-and-seek in the dark.

He writes about this in one of his earliest short stories 'The End of The Party' (1929), and it recurs in a particularly dramatic context in his screenplay for Carol Reed's *The Fallen Idol*. The reason for it being his favourite game was, he said, because it contained 'the agreeable ingredient of fear'.[17] Greene always found the emotion of fear seductive (he links it explicitly with love in *The Human Factor*): it keeps at bay the enemy of boredom and may explain why he was so drawn to trouble spots in his adult life as inspiration for his novels. Nevertheless, he made a crucial distinction between fear and terror. The former might be seductive but the latter is something from which one tries to escape, screaming. He would undoubtedly have understood that extraordinary passage in the second chapter of Dickens's *Great Expectations* where the narrator, Pip recalls his state of mind in childhood, and which seems close to Greene's mood for much of his childhood and adolescence: 'I have often thought that few people know what secrecy there is in the young, under terror. No matter how unreasonable the terror, so that it be terror.' The 'secrecy' of 'the young under terror', to borrow Dickens's phrase, was particularly to afflict Greene at school, having a profound effect on him and inflicting a psychological injury that he was to repay, and repair, in his fiction.

The nightmare began in his thirteenth year when he became a boarder at the school at which his father was a headmaster. His father's study and the school were separated by a green baize door. When he went through this door, the terror assaulted him with the force of a hurricane. Small wonder that the motif of crossing borders is such a strong one in Greene (think, for example, of his powerful short story, 'Across The Bridge'): it all relates back to the green baize door, on one side of which was domestic security and, on the other side, enemy territory. He felt like an alien in a strange land whose language he does not quite understand (another constant motif in Greene, from Holly in *The Third Man* to Henry in *Travels With My Aunt*). He felt not only like a foreigner but also like a suspect, a hunted creature. To Marie-Francoise Allain, he explained: 'I couldn't side with the boys without betraying my father, and they regarded me like a collaborator in a foreign territory.'[18] In *A Sort of Life*, he wrote: 'I was like the son of a quisling in a country under occupation. I was surrounded by the forces of the resistance and yet I couldn't join them without betraying my father and brother.'[19] Of a naturally shy disposition (close friends like Michael Meyer and casual acquaintances like Igor Stravinsky have commented similarly on that aspect of his temperament) and with a slight lisp in speaking that made him self-conscious and exaggerated the shyness (even later in life when famous, he was sensitive enough about his speech to ask Francois Truffaut to change a line in *Day for Night* so that it would not expose his inability to say his 'r's), Greene must have suffered agonies at this situation. It made him secretive; it made it difficult for him to form friendships; it made him deeply unhappy.

There were contributory factors to his distress. For someone of his shyness and sensitivity, the lack of privacy was not just a trial but a continual torment. 'No moment of the night,' he wrote, 'was free from noise, a cough, a snore, a fart'.[20] One could be excused for thinking that Greene's image of hell at this time was of a lavatory without locks, because he alludes to this deprivation not only in the autobiography but also in his concluding essay in *The Old School* (1934) ('even locks on the lavatory doors would have been something') and in his prologue to *The Lawless Roads*. 'One began to believe in heaven because one believed in hell,' he wrote, 'but for a long time it was only hell one could picture with a certain intimacy – the pitchpine partitions in dormitories where everybody was never quiet at the same time, lavatories without locks...'[21] This experience of institutional life was to accentuate Greene's preference for the life of a loner and also to sharpen his life-long hatred of authority, of institutionalised obedience. His instinctive sympathy was to be for the oppressed, as he saw himself, for those who lie outside the boundaries of state approval; his literary instinct was to be the piece of grit in the State machinery. It is no surprise that he so admired and enjoyed Lindsay Anderson's blistering attack on the public-school system in his film, *If...* (1968): it contains something of his own sardonic contempt for the system.

In his book, *The Old School*, Greene includes an essay by W.H. Auden on his old school, Gresham's School, which has a particularly interesting section on what Auden saw as its oppressive code of honour, which encouraged informing on boys who broke the rules of no swearing, smoking or indecent language or behaviour. 'It meant that the whole of our moral life was based on fear,' Auden wrote, 'or fear of the community, not to mention the temptation it offered to the natural informer, and fear is not a healthy basis. It makes one furtive and dishonest and adventurous.' He adds, in a droll aside that enlarges on the political significance of this: 'The best reason I have for opposing Fascism is that at school I lived in a Fascist state.'[22] This may have struck a powerful chord with Greene who, as we have noted, was bullied at school by two boys, Carter and Watson. The bullying consisted of a psychological torture that reduced Greene to a state of near-nervous breakdown, attempts at suicide and running away from school. What is not so well known is the fact that Norman Sherry was to uncover: namely, that, after three years of mental torment, Greene was to inform on Carter to his father. Carter was withdrawn from the school and his later career never recovered. (Again it makes one think of Greene's fascination with the film, *These Three*: what happened to the evil child, Mary after her 'lie' had been discovered? What kind of punishment did she receive? What kind of adult would she have become?) As already noted, in *A Sort of Life*, when he describes his accidental meeting with Watson in Sierra Leone in middle age, he intimates that Carter had since died, though Sherry says that this was not actually the case: at that time,

Lionel Carter was still alive and was to live until 1971, shortly before his 'exposure' in Greene's autobiography. It is tempting to wonder whether Greene knew this. Was he concealing his guilt at having informed on his tormentor? It is Sherry's view that Greene never forgave himself for this, that it broke a basic code of never divulging a secret. The net impact of this experience, he argues, was twofold. 'In school was born his deep concern for the underdog (for so he felt himself to be), the hunted man and the downtrodden everywhere,' Sherry wrote. The second effect was the compulsion to court danger. 'This became the basic pattern of his mind,' he writes, 'moving from domestic existence to the dangers of the world, ... because it meant he was returning to his experience of the Carters out there in the dangerous world ... Greene had betrayed someone at sixteen, become unwittingly an informer, and he sought in his world confirmation of betrayal almost as the central characteristic of man'.[23]

Perhaps the most desolate expression of the conjunction between childhood and betrayal in Greene is in the short story 'The Basement Room', where a young boy becomes privy to the love affair of the butler Baines. He will disclose the existence of Baines's mistress to the police after Baines's wife has died in mysterious circumstances, thus implicating Baines in the cause of her death and betraying a man who has been kind to him. On his deathbed many years later, he will still recall the phrase which has ensnared him in the interrogation ('Who is she?') and set the path that his life will take. 'Life fell on him with savagery,' Greene wrote, 'and you couldn't blame him if he never faced it again in sixty years'.[24] Quite apart from the story's remarkable anticipation of L.P. Hartley's great novel, *The Go-Between*, which anticipates in some of its details and theme (notably the situation of an old man recollecting a traumatic act of childhood betrayal which has had a determining influence on the adult he has grown into), it is also fascinating for its imagery. What separates Philip's innocent world of childhood from the adult world of passion and hate is a green baize door. 'He had no appetite,' Greene writes, when he has returned home from the tea room where he has blundered unknowingly into Baines's tryst with Emmy and Baines has forsworn him to secrecy. 'He strained his ears for Mrs Baines's coming, for the sound of voices, but the basement held its secrets; the green baize door shut off that world.'[25] When he blunders through it, however, he will precociously encounter a nightmare world that Greene himself endured when going through a similar setting. In *The Dangerous Edge*, Lambert (1975) shrewdly picked up the symbolism of the green baize door and applied it penetratingly to Greene's own situation. On opening the door, the child, Lambert writes, 'goes downstairs to confront the mystery of an adult passion and the violent quarrel that creates a death. The child never recovers from the early experience, growing up into a cold haunted dilettante. Greene never recovers either, but grows up into a novelist. The writer becomes a fugitive from the emptiness and boredom of Philip who spent all his courage and remained forever crying in the dark'.[26] The boy is Greene as he might have become, the story a sort of exorcism, an evocation of a world the novelist can explore but the man must escape.

When one thinks of Greene's representation of childhood in his novels, one's first thought is probably of Pinkie in *Brighton Rock* and the dreadful Saturday nights and 'the frightening weekly exercise of his parents which he watched from his single bed'.[27] He will cling to his virginity like his bottle of vitriol: killing will be his consummation. 'He trailed the clouds of his own glory after him': Greene writes in Wordsworthian mockery, 'hell lay about him in his infancy. He was ready for more deaths'.[28] The insistent reference to him in the text as 'The Boy' suggests that he has never escaped from this childhood torment, being part devil, part lost soul. His progress as an adult is, to borrow Charlotte Bronte's phrase about her sister Emily's character Heathcliff, 'an arrow-straight course to perdition'. Yet even as Pinkie heads towards an unavoidable hellfire and damnation, Greene makes us aware of the human torment beneath the villainy: he can empathise with the pain. This is particularly true of the terrifying yet unbearably poignant description of his death, where he is burned by his own vitriol and shrinks back to the frightened child from where all the emotional poison of his heart and mind has festered and flowed: 'He looked half his size, doubled up in appalling agony, it was as if the flames had literally got him and he shrank – shrank into a schoolboy flying in panic and pain . . .' Immediately before then, Rose had seen his face that 'was like a child's, badgered, confused, betrayed: fake years slipped away – he was whisked back towards the unhappy playground'.[29]

In *England Made Me*, Greene offers a different portrait of arrested development related to childhood and school. The central character,

Anthony Farrant is imprisoned in the past through his undisclosed incestuous feelings for his twin sister, Kate, that thwart his emotional development, and by an antiquated set of public-school values that seem socially anachronistic and hopelessly inadequate for dealing with the political ruthlessness of the modern age. His gentlemanly appeasement and dilettante deviousness take on an implied political dimension, a metaphor for England's political childishness in comprehending and dealing with the impending European horror. But in some ways one of the most compelling moments occurs in the middle of Kate's stream-of-consciousness meanderings as she lies beside the sleeping figure of her lover Krogh while her thoughts are all of Anthony and their childhood together. 'Those we love we forget,' she muses, 'it is those we betray we remember'.[30] It could almost be Greene himself having nightmares about the dreaded Carter. It is only in his later works that the child becomes a more playful or positive symbol. One thinks of the exasperated innocence of Felipe in *The Fallen Idol*, Greene's more upbeat screen treatment of the material of 'The Basement Room'; or the chubby-faced mischievous little boy, Hansl (Herbert Halbik) in *The Third Man* whose prime joy in life seems to be to get Holly into trouble, almost as if he were a prototype of the young Harry Lime. One thinks of the tender straightforwardness of the children's stories that he wrote to be illustrated by Dorothy Craigie. The love of the private detective Parkis for his son in *The End of the Affair* provides a welcome relief from the adult anguish elsewhere; and the lightness of tone in *Our Man in Havana* is partly attributable to the motivation for Wormold's treachery, which stems not from enervating adult greed or passion but from his love for his vivacious daughter. The most moving expression of parental love in Greene is arguably in *The Human Factor*, where the boy becomes the focus of Maurice and Sarah's life in a way that transcends all notions of national loyalty. 'We have our own country,' says Sarah. 'You and I and Sam. You've never betrayed that country, Maurice.'[31]

Yet memories of childhood never leave Greene, and it is curious how full his work is of childhood imagery, sometimes in quite incongruous contexts (like the reference mentioned earlier to the 'Old Boy' when discussing Humphrey Bogart's characterisation of the gangster in *Dead End*) and in a manner that is quite unlike any other major twentieth-century novelist I can think of. When Pinkie is attacked by the razor-gang at the racetrack in *Brighton Rock*, Greene writes: 'he was filled with horror and astonishment as if one of the bullied brats at school had stabbed first with the dividers'.[32] (Remember that one of Pinkie's very last memories is to whisk him back to that 'unhappy playground'.) As Cunningham (1989) notes, Greene is at least balanced here in suggesting that the one thing that unites every school is the prevalence of Original Sin, that evil was not only the product of the private education system but could also manifest itself in the Council School yard.[33] But the most striking thing is the way the sensation of pain seems immediately and ineluctably to summon up memories of childhood and school, of bullies and sadists, and victims. Characters who are particularly marked by their childhood or school experience – like Pinkie, like Anthony in *England Made Me*, like Raven in *A Gun for Sale* – significantly are facially scarred, the outward symbol of an inner emotional wound. In *The Heart of the Matter*, Greene has an unusual but telling image for the guilty but sorrowful Portugese captain of the *Esperanca* who gives himself away with a repeated nervous gesture of wiping his eyes with the back of his hand – 'like a child', Greene writes, 'an unattractive child, the fat boy of the school'.[34] It is an image that conveys a real sense of vulnerability but also gives a glimpse of the unhappy child within the man's body. In Greene's mind, it seems to me, there was no real demarcation between the child and the man, that one could easily be located in the other. The derivation of that idea comes from the green baize door of his childhood, which so flimsily separated home from school, security from sadness, family from fear. In *The Heart of the Matter*, Harris muses about his unhappy schooldays. 'To start off happy,' he says. 'It must make an awful difference afterwards. Why it might become a habit, mightn't it?'[35] After his own schooldays, happiness never became a habit for Greene, and in later years, he said, when a school theme began to form in his mind as a possible subject for a novel, he escaped to a leper colony in the Congo rather than be forced to revisit that area of experience. Nevertheless, he did recognise that complete escape from those formative years was impossible: one could only hope to make constructive use of the memory of them, even of the pain and unhappiness. 'We always live our childhood again,' wrote the Estonian poet, Jaan Kaplinski, before adding a sentiment with which Greene would have undoubtedly concurred: 'Even then, we don't want it back.'[36]

8
Poets of Criminality and Conscience: Greene and Hitchcock

Alfred Hitchcock, Graham Greene: the comparison can't be evaded for long.

– Raymond Durgnat[1]

I felt the book just wouldn't survive his touch.

– Graham Greene[2]

In his Foreword to the most recent edition of Quentin Falk's indispensable book on Greene and the cinema, *Travels in Greeneland*, writer-director, Neil Jordan makes the following comment about Greene as a film critic: 'He was one of the most incisive to have written in England, even given his strange miasma about the work of Alfred Hitchcock. And there must be another book to be written ... about the lack of contact between these two poets of English criminality and bad conscience.'[3] This chapter is an exploration of what Jordan aptly calls Greene's 'strange miasma' (it went beyond being a blind spot) on the subject of Hitchcock's films and what it might reveal about Greene's artistic personality. Jordan's comment is an invitation to re-examine this comparison[4] because, as Raymond Durgnat says quite rightly in the first of the chapter's epigraphs, the connection between the two is so insistent and unavoidable that there is something distinctly perverse about Greene's consistent denigration of Hitchcock. In his review of Hitchcock's *Secret Agent* for *The Spectator* (15 May 1936), Greene had complained of what he called the director's 'inadequate sense of reality ... he has no sense of life. His films consist of a series of small "amusing" melodramatic situations...they mean nothing: they lead to nothing'. Although he later confessed to Quentin Falk a liking for Hitchcock's *Notorious* (1946), he basically held to this opinion of Hitchcock, repeating it in his introduction to the publication of his collected film criticism, *The Pleasure Dome* in 1972.

Greene's aversion to Hitchcock does not seem to have been reciprocated. Indeed, one of Hitchcock's famous anthologies of suspense stories, his 1947 *Fireside Book of Suspense*, which he edited and introduced, includes a rather rare story of Greene's 'The News in English' (1940), which Greene did not include in his *Collected Short Stories* of 1972 and only reappeared in book form in one of his final publications, *The Last Word* (1990). It is worth remembering also (it is not often mentioned by Greene biographers) that Hitchcock was considering Greene as a possible screenwriter for his film *I Confess* (1953) on a subject that would seem to have been right up his street, turning on the inviolability of the Catholic confessional even when, as in this case, the priest who has heard the confession of a murderer himself becomes the chief suspect for that crime. Yet, Greene turned him down.[5] And when Hitchcock attempted to acquire the film rights of *Our Man in Havana* in 1958, Greene refused to sell them to him. It seems as if Greene were actively determined to keep a distance between him and Hitchcock, making an almost self-conscious endeavour to suppress any hint of a connection. Did he protest too much? It does seem profoundly ironic that his one screen appearance as an actor was in a film by the man who had done more than any other to elevate Hitchcock's artistic status – namely, Truffaut. In the introduction to his celebrated book-length interview with Hitchcock, Truffaut claimed that Hitchcock's work ranked alongside the work of 'such artists of anxiety as Kafka, Dostoevsky and Poe'.[6] He could have added Greene to that list.

Hitchcock has been a kind of *leitmotif* throughout this book. The parallels and analogies between him and Greene might initially seem coincidental and even incidental, but they seem to me so numerous as to warrant comment and to suggest almost a secret kinship between the two, which in turn might illuminate aspects of their artistic personalities. For Greene, it might be a little more than kinship, and he has been a little less than kind. Yet, in spite of their widely differing temperaments and background, they seem to have seen humanity in strikingly similar ways. The manner of their exploration of human psychology has also shared certain characteristics, as has the evolution of their respective reputations.

To explore some parallels first. To begin with, their development was rather similar. During the 1930s, both made their respective reputations with quirky, characterful explorations of English crime. Greene establishes his reputation as a master with the crime thriller, *Brighton Rock* (1938); Hitchcock confirms his status as England's finest director and 'master of suspense' with *The 39 Steps* (1935) and *The Lady Vanishes* (1938). During the 1940s and 1950s, they both acquire celebrity status and their work expands into an international phase. Greene exploits exotic locations and explores political themes in works such as *The Heart of the Matter* (1948), *The Quiet American* (1955) and *Our Man in Havana* (1958); Hitchcock ranges across American politics and psyche in *Notorious, Strangers on A Train* (1951), *Rear Window* (1954), and *North by Northwest* (1959). In the 1970s, both revisit the England of their past, recreating a kind of anachronistic thriller in the style of the 1930s, but tinged with a modern harshness – in Greene's case, *The Human Factor* (1978), in Hitchcock's case, *Frenzy* (1972).

Both have their political phase. Greene's anti-Americanism is certainly more corrosive than Hitchcock's but in Hitchcock films like *Notorious* and *North by Northwest*, one can sense a Greene-like sardonic critique of the Secret Service and a fear of the kind of global conspiracy and paranoid political game-playing that can render the individual helpless. Greene's political sensibilities are more radical and finely tuned than Hitchcock's, and his nose for the next political trouble-spot was unrivalled ('when I hear that Graham is going off to visit some part of the globe', Alec Guinness used to say jokingly, 'I will avoid the place like the plague because that means that a revolution or war is bound to break out there soon.'[7]). Yet Hitchcock's political films are a subgenre of their own that are only now beginning to attract closer attention for their political insights. One thinks of his 'terrorist' films like *Sabotage* and the two versions of *The Man Who Knew Too Much* (1934 and 1956); his wartime dramas, *Foreign Correspondent* (1940) and *Lifeboat* (1944), with their urgent contemporary messages; the two films he made for the British Ministry of Information in support of the French Resistance, *Bon Voyage* and *Adventure Malagache* (both 1944); *Torn Curtain* (1966), a strange Faustian allegory of

American meddling abroad, made at the time of the Vietnam War; and his account of the Cuban missile crisis, *Topaz* (1969), a much more sombre affair than Greene's prophetic novel on the subject, *Our Man in Havana*.

Other parallels can be mentioned. Greene used to list some of his novels as 'entertainments' (that is, novels with a heady combination of plot, melodrama and suspense, rather than a more overtly serious purpose, be it moral or political): it was not until the late 1960s and *Travels With My Aunt* that he discontinued this practice. It would not be hard to divide Hitchcock's work in a similar way, the 'entertainments' including most of the English films and American works like *To Catch A Thief* (1955), *The Trouble With Harry* (1955) and *North by Northwest*, the serious including more sombre psychological and even religious exercises such as *Sabotage* (1936), *I Confess, The Wrong Man* (1957) and *Vertigo* (1958). (Perhaps it might be said that, in both cases, the distinction seems equally artificial: Greene abandoned the term on realising that his 'entertainments' dealt with the same themes as his 'serious' work and the 'serious' texts were as entertaining as the 'entertainments' – the same could be said of Hitchcock.) Greene relaxes in his short stories; Hitchcock relaxes in his short TV films; nevertheless, in both cases, characteristic themes and flourishes emerge. Greene has 'a blinding terror of birds';[8] Hitchcock makes the ultimate film about such terror, *The Birds* (1963). Greene is much inspired by his dreams, saying that short stories such as 'Dream of a Strange Land' and 'The Root of All Evil' were written as a direct result of dreams; Hitchcock films like *Spellbound* (1945) and *Marnie* (1964) are intensely dreamlike and have a Greene-like fascination with the mysteries of the unconscious mind. Greene writes train novels, like *Stamboul Train* (1932); Hitchcock makes train movies like *Number Seventeen* (1932), *The 39 Steps* and *The Lady Vanishes* (1938). As Peter Conrad has pointed out, Hitchcock's *Secret Agent* 'ends aboard the train to Constantinople; Graham Greene's thriller, *Stamboul Train* takes the same journey'.[9] Stephen Wall has seen similarities in conception and characterisation between *Stamboul Train* and *The Lady Vanishes* and referred to the 'Hitchcockian opening of *The Ministry of Fear* in which an apparently reassuring fête in a London square turns sinister.'[10] And Durgnat (1974) has observed that even the titles of their work in some instances – *Secret Agent, Confidential Agent* – seem interchangeable, and that, if one could define the character of Hitchcock's output in a phrase, one might be tempted to call it a 'ministry of fear'.[11]

One might add that the development of their reputations has been similar. Patronisingly referred to by the critical establishment as 'old masters', there is still the nagging sense of a certain underestimation. If Hitchcock is the greatest Hollywood director never to have won a directing Oscar, Greene is the greatest modern novelist never to have won the Nobel Prize. In both cases, one could argue that they themselves might have been partially to blame, Hitchcock carefully projecting a rather reassuring image of himself of comic and craftsman that might have distracted attention from the profundities of his work, Greene also colluding in an image of himself – the detached spectator of life's failure – that did less than justice to the range of his capacities and compassion.

All of these may seem rather superficial similarities, a set of coincidences that do not, however, have much of substance to say about either artist. My own feeling is that the sheer number of parallels between the two of them, even on a surface level, is at least intriguing; and this goes still further when one starts to examine influences and dramatic situations. For example, it is curious that both of them felt an enormous attachment to J.M. Barrie's play, *Mary Rose*. Greene describes his admiration in *A Sort of Life*, saying 'it had left behind a sense of fading poetry like a scent in a drawer and of deeply buried emotions inexplicable without the professional aid of Kenneth Richmond'.[12] Hitchcock described his interest in the material at some length to Francois Truffaut when he was planning to make the film after *Marnie*; his biographer, Donald Spoto was to describe Hitchcock's failure to make it as 'perhaps the single greatest disappointment of his creative life'.[13] What is extraordinary (the thought gives me goose pimples) is that it is quite possible that they saw the same production: Hitchcock saw it in 1920 with Fay Compton in the main role, and Greene mentions that he saw it with his parents – by the time of the later productions during the decade, he would be married. The theme is a haunting one of tragic disappearance and then an almost miraculous return after death that nevertheless brings trauma and tragedy in its wake: both Greene and Hitchcock will offer their own intensely personal transformations of this theme – in *The End of The Affair* and *Vertigo*, respectively. Agreeing with Truffaut on the sadness of the subject matter, Hitchcock said that for him the main theme was: 'If the dead were to come back, what would you do with them?'[14] It is a statement that eerily recalls for me that moment in *The Third Man*, when Harry Lime – another dead person who miraculously re-materialises – stares down from the Great Wheel at the dots of humanity below and, after proclaiming a belief in God, murmurs: 'The dead are happier dead. They don't miss much here, poor devils.'

Another enthusiasm and influence they had in common was the writer, John Buchan. 'He was the first,' wrote Greene, 'to realise the enormous dramatic value of adventure in familiar surroundings happening to unadventurous people'. In the same essay, he quotes a line from Buchan's *The Power House*: 'Now I saw how thin is the protection of civilisation.'[15] Taken together, those two statements could be almost a definition of Hitchcockian cinema, which plunges ordinary man into extraordinary situations and where the most seemingly harmless of settings – a shower, a fairground, a prairie stop, a children's playground, the home – become charged with menace, as the forces of chaos invade the world of order and the everyday and undermine our complacency. Conversely, a comment of Hitchcock's about Buchan makes one think of Greene. 'Buchan was a strong influence a long time before I undertook *The 39 Steps*,' he told Truffaut. 'What I find appealing in Buchan's work is his understatement of highly dramatic ideas.'[16] That could be directly applied to Greene, who had a horror of melodrama and overstatement and whose most powerful events are often obliquely described (like the bomb in *The Quiet American* that not only goes off in the middle of a square but in the middle of a sentence, which you have to re-read to grasp what has happened) or simply left to resonate with deadly implication (like the devastating final sentence of *Brighton Rock*). Another thing that Greene and Hitchcock share with Buchan is the dramatic situation of 'the hunted man', which preoccupied them both: in Greene novels such as *The Man Within*, *The Power and the Glory* and *The Human Factor*; and in at least a dozen Hitchcock films, from *The 39 Steps* to *Saboteur*, from *Shadow of a Doubt* to *North By Northwest*.

It seems therefore oddly perverse of Greene to dislike Hitchcock's filming of Buchan. 'How inexcusably he spoilt *The Thirty-Nine Steps*,' he wrote of Hitchcock's film version,[17] a judgement few would now endorse, since most seem to feel that the film was an immeasurable improvement on the story, including, according to Hitchcock, Buchan himself. It seems even more perverse when one recalls that, in *The Third Man*, Greene constructs a situation that is straight out of Hitchcock's film – the hero stumbling into a hall and being required to give an unexpected, impromptu lecture – but which has no precedent in the Buchan novel. Indeed, there is a way in which one can see *The Third Man* as a very Hitchcockian film. The use of the Great Wheel in Vienna as a metaphor for the wheel of modern history against which the individual looks small and puny has a symbolic similarity to Hitchcock's use of the windmill in his anti-Nazi melodrama, *Foreign Correspondent*. Similarly, as Raymond Durgnat pointed out, the 'transference of guilt' theme, which Eric Rohmer and Claude Chabrol identified as a key motif in Hitchcock in their ground-breaking monograph on the director in 1957, could just as easily be identified in *The Third Man*: as Durgnat says, 'it fits every requirement which Chabrol and Rohmer think are specific to Hitchcock, particularly the very obvious "transference of guilt" between Orson Welles, Joseph Cotten and the suitably chastised spectator, who has identified with the latter'.[18] A parallel scene in Hitchcock would be the one between Guy (Farley Granger) and Bruno (Robert Walker) in *Strangers on A Train* after the latter has murdered Guy's wife and is expecting Guy to join his great enterprise, fulfil his part of the bargain by murdering Bruno's father: the audience is torn between admiration for, and being appalled by, Bruno's audacity and charisma (like Lime's) and irritation at the hero's glum normalcy (like Holly's) which will lead him to an act of ignoble betrayal. 'I'm very much concerned with dualism and the good and evil that exists in everyone to some degree,' said Patricia Highsmith about her novel. So was Greene (who wrote appreciatively of Highsmith): so was Hitchcock.

The connections multiply. Spoto (1975) has usefully compared *Shadow of a Doubt* with *Brighton Rock*,[19] suggesting that Hitchcock's heroine, Charley and Greene's heroine, Rose are similar characters – untempted and untried individuals forced to undergo a moral education by confronting an evil soul-mate, Hitchcock's Uncle Charlie and Greene's Pinkie, who are both demons and lost souls. The parallel is reinforced by a certain similarity of mise-en-scène, where a key scene between the two characters in both works takes place in a cheap café. Uncle Charlie's homicidal rage against the complacent 'merry widows' whom he murders is also not dissimilar to Pinkie's – and Greene's – loathing of the earthy vulgar shallowness of Ida Arnold. An equally potent parallel to *Brighton Rock* is *Strangers on A Train*. Hitchcock's Bruno has all of Pinkie's Puritanism and instinctive equation of sexuality and evil; and the film shares Greene's metaphor of the fairground as a site of libidinous chaos, particularly emphasised in the film version of Greene's novel. Indeed, if one moves on to the film of *Brighton Rock*, the fascinating and controversial ending, as conceived by Greene, seems to me like nothing else in the cinema other than the ending of *Vertigo*. In both films, their loved ones have fallen to their deaths; and, in both cases, the last word is given to a nun invoking God's mercy. Hitchcock's Scottie has been cured of his vertigo; Greene's Rose has been saved from the worst horror of all by the record needle sticking in the groove on the words 'I love you'. But in both cases, one asks: what about the shot, as it were, after the film's closure? As Greene said, Rose will at some time move the needle on; and, although Scottie's vertigo is conquered, he is staring into an abyss so terrible that the next stage might be his fall.

Or take this description by Greene in *A Sort of Life* at a particular stage in his life when he was in a distraught state of mind: 'My nerves horribly on edge, that feeling of lurking madness, of something swelling in the brain and wanting to burst, every sound, however small, made by anyone else, the clink of a plate or a fork, *piercing the brain like a knife*.' [my italics][20] Could there be a more precise description than that of the mood evoked in one of Hitchcock's most famous scenes – the 'knife' scene in *Blackmail*? The heroine has stabbed to death a man who has been trying to rape her: at home the next morning, she becomes acutely sensitive to everything around her, Hitchcock brilliantly seeking out external expressive means to convey the heroine's inner tension (which she is trying to conceal), and to show how the killing is still preying on her mind. He achieves his effect through using sound subjectively, so that the heroine becomes hypersensitive to the word 'knife', the word itself seeming to stab through the indecipherable blur of conversation and press unbearably on her stretched nerves. What is fascinating there is not only the fact that Hitchcock realises visually and aurally, precisely the kind of mental torment that Greene is describing verbally: it is the fact that they use the same imagery to do so.

Perhaps the two fundamental parallels between them can be seen in terms of narrative and religion. No one could dispute that, in their respective fields, they were master story-tellers. 'I think he's brilliant but erratic in his logic,' was the nearest Greene came to complimenting Hitchcock[21] (something that could equally apply to Greene), but both knew how to mesmerise their audiences through sheer narrative momentum and inventiveness. In Greene's case, the question arises: why are his novels so compulsively readable yet the films of them sometimes listless and lacking in narrative vitality? Greene believed it was because one cannot tell a story from the single point of view of one character in a film as one can in a novel and, because of that, coherence and concentration were dissipated. He wanted the first film version of *The End of the Affair* to employ the first-person camera technique that Robert Montgomery had experimented with in his 1948 film of Raymond Chandler's *Lady in the Lake*, where the camera is in effect the hero's eyes and we never see his face (except in a mirror), but the technique had baffled and irritated audiences and was not repeated. Ironically, what Greene seemed to be after was the kind of modified subjective point-of-view filming of which Hitchcock had proved himself a master – in the first third of *Psycho*, the first two-thirds of *Vertigo* and the whole of *Rear Window*. Technically, there is surely a connection between the way Greene makes us identify with the hunted man, Hale in *Brighton Rock*, so that we feel disorientated when he is killed off, and the way Hitchcock compels our identification with Marion Crane (Janet Leigh) in the opening part of *Psycho*, so that her murder in the shower seems doubly shocking and leaves us temporarily adrift in the narrative.

The second fundamental parallel between them is their Catholicism. No need to demonstrate its importance in Greene's novels, but it might not be so familiar to spectators of Hitchcock's films. Like Greene, Hitchcock was a deeply religious man and this shows in the imagery in some of his films at moments of great intensity. For example, there is a scene in *The Wrong Man* when the hero Manny Balestrero (Henry Fonda) prays for relief from his troubles and, at that moment, the real criminal 'miraculously' steps forward to superimpose his presence on Manny's face prior to committing the crime that will clear the hero's name. As Truffaut said: 'It seems unlikely to me that anyone but a Catholic would have handled Henry Fonda's prayer scene as you did.'[22] There is the ghostly appearance of the nun that causes the guilty woman to fall to her death at the end of *Vertigo* and whose words seal the theme of what seems to me Hitchcock's supreme masterpiece, 'God have mercy.' The whole dramatic structure of *I Confess*, as previously mentioned, is built around the confidentiality of the confessional, which seems slowly and perversely to be tightening a noose around the priest's neck. If, in general terms, one had to define the influence of Catholicism on the work of both artists, one might echo Truffaut's feeling that Hitchcock's work is 'strongly permeated by the concept of original sin, and of man's guilt',[23] and Gavin Lambert's feeling that Greene has a 'Catholic fascination with the ignoble.'[24]

Let me make two specific comparisons. Although Hitchcock failed to secure the film rights to *Our Man in Havana*, it is often remarked that he did eventually make his film about the Cuban missile crisis, *Topaz* (1969), which turned out to be one of the dullest movies of his career. What has not been noticed so often is that the film he made instead of *Our Man in Havana*, namely *North by Northwest* – which, in a different context, I have also compared with *A Burnt-Out Case* – has a lot in common with the Greene narrative, almost as if Hitchcock were defiantly transplanting it to another context. Both texts are light in tone, with darker colourations, and both about ordinary men in increasingly extraordinary and dangerous situations. In Greene's novel, a vacuum cleaner salesman, Wormold, is exploited by MI6, embodied in the film by Noel Coward; in Hitchcock's film, the hero Thornhill is exploited by the CIA, represented by Leo G. Carroll ('FBI, CIA – we're all part of the same alphabet soup,' comments Carroll). For mercenary reasons, Wormold prolongs his deception as a spy by submitting drawings of suspicious military installations that are actually vacuum cleaners. For reasons of survival and romance, Thornhill continues his deception by assuming the identity of someone who does not exist but who does have dandruff. Both are sophisticated comedy thrillers that nevertheless have an unusually mature and dark Cold War subtext about the political ruthlessness of the State and the expendability of the individual. Yet, whereas Carol Reed's film of Greene's novel was rather heavy in its humour, Hitchcock's film was spry and sparkling, as if to show how it could have been done. Contrary to Greene's view, the Hitchcock touch was precisely what was needed.

The other comparison takes us back to the beginning of the chapter and Neil Jordan's comparison of Greene and Hitchcock, for I wonder if, in making the new screen version of *The End of the Affair* (1999), Jordan became aware of how similar the narrative is in many ways to

Hitchcock's *Vertigo*? One could summarise the plot of Greene's novel as follows: a husband hires a friend via a private eye to spy on his wife, because she has been behaving strangely. Unbeknown to the husband, the man has fallen in love with the wife. In the middle of the affair, one of them seems to have died: the partner is distraught and re-evaluates her life. But the person is not dead, and is hurt and traumatised by the loved one's disappearance. With just a little tweaking, this could be a plot summary of *Vertigo* too, another love affair involving spying, duplicity, adultery, possessiveness, in the middle of which one of them seems to have died but then reappears. The effect in both is to throw the relationship awry and the narrative also, because a story which we have been following from one point of view becomes something else when seen in the second half from a different perspective. In both cases, the woman's 'confession' becomes a crucial narrative crux; and both gather to religious conclusions where a priest plays a key role in the novel and a nun in the film. Jordan's film of the Greene novel might seem a tragic love story and Hitchcock's film more of a thriller, but they are both death-haunted stories of romantic obsession with a strong religious undercurrent. They each feature a hero who tries to free himself from the past, who is in the grip of a love so intense as to be close to hatred, and who at the end is precariously balanced at the edge of a spiritual void and trying to still a haunted heart. Given his admiration for the film, it seems to me quite likely that *Vertigo* was somewhere in Neil Jordan's mind when he was making *The End of the Affair*; could Greene have been in Hitchcock's mind when making *Vertigo*? It is intriguing that the two were in contact round about the time of the making and premiere of Hitchcock's film, but I am more inclined to think it less a case of influence as a case of two artists with similar sensibilities coincidentally exploring similar themes in a way that is both profoundly individual but also shows an almost instinctive, subconscious connection.

We are left, then, with two tantalising questions. The first relates to a simple matter of aesthetics. Although I have assembled here a mass of material that seems to me to point clear links between two of the greatest popular artists of the last century in their respective fields, this still invites the question: does it matter? Does it make any significant difference in our perception of Greene or Hitchcock? My own feeling is that it does; and it also makes a difference to our perception of the relation between literature and film. Back in 1969, in his seminal book on film aesthetics, *Signs and Meaning in the Cinema*, Peter Wollen mapped out his view of some future projects for the then relatively new area of Film Studies, one of which, he claimed, was that 'we need comparisons with authors in the other arts: Ford with Fenimore Cooper, for example, or Hawks with Faulkner'.[25] More than thirty years on, this potentially fertile area of study has still not been developed (there is definitely a book to be written, for example, comparing Chaplin with Charles Dickens): the fields of Literary and Film Studies have been more often antagonistic than complementary. Yet I agree with Leonard Bernstein, in the first of his masterly Harvard lectures entitled 'The Unanswered Question', when he said that 'the best way to "know" a thing is in the context of another discipline'.[26] This has particular relevance to Greene who, as I have argued elsewhere in the book, seemed consciously to deploy what he had picked up from the critical activity of watching and reviewing films to solve some of his problems as a novelist. How much of that is indebted to Hitchcock is a moot point, but Raymond Durgnat certainly felt that the connection between the two extended to technique as well as theme. 'Greene and Hitchcock reveal affinities also on the level of style,' he wrote. 'Both combine an astonishing expertise at rapid narrative with a sensitivity to atmospherics and details which it is not at all absurd to see as an adaptation of the stream-of-consciousness tradition ... And in both cases, it is a creative one since stream-of-consciousness, in focusing on perceptual detail, often has the greatest difficulty in eliminating detail sufficiently to deal with the articulation of significant dramatic events'.[27] This characterisation of the two styles as having the perceptual sophistication of stream-of-consciousness whist retaining the significant specificity of plot and place seems to me both accurate and astute; and would explain why the work of both men, in a quite remarkable way, seems to satisfy simultaneously the tastes of the mass audience and the critical connoisseur.

The larger question remains and it is the one with which we began: given the propinquity of the two artists, why did Greene have what Neil Jordan has called this 'strange miasma' about Hitchcock's work? It is all the more striking since, aside from his dismissal of *The Bride of Frankenstein* in his first film column for *The Spectator* (5 July 1935), his reservations about Hitchcock are virtually the only judgments of his as a film critic that have not stood the test of time. Admittedly, he was only dealing with the earlier English films but he never changed his mind even after what is regarded as Hitchcock's greatest period, from 1951 to 1964. My suspicion is that it was the equivalent of his decision not to read Conrad for thirty years: he feared the contamination of influence, which he therefore had to keep at arm's length through irony or denigration. To Greene, Hitchcock may have appeared to be another 'Other' – like the other Graham Greene who seems to be stalking him at the end of *Ways of Escape* and may be the real thing, or like the figure in a favourite poem of Greene's, Edward Thomas's 'The Other':

> I travelled fast, in hopes I should
> Outrun that other. What to do
> When caught, I planned not. I pursued
> To prove the likeness and, if true,
> To watch until myself I knew.[28]

Greene would surely have seen this connection in the 1930s; would have wanted to 'outrun' the other; but would have baulked at the prospect, as it were, of confronting the other in order to know himself better. On the contrary, Greene's resistance to Hitchcock is comparable to Conrad's hatred of Dostoevsky: it is not the dismissal of a nonentity but a fear of his power, and a fear of an encroachment on territory he had marked out for himself. Small wonder Greene would have stood out against working with Hitchcock on *Our Man in Havana*. To the critic, it might have seemed a match made in Heaven: to Greene, the prospect might have seemed less of a collaboration than a confrontation with a disturbing Double. But they remain the most fascinating complementary couple of literature and film.

Conclusion: Forgotten Memories

When his implacable blue eyes focus on one of us, they are trans-
parently seeing something else. His brows knit instead, his jowls
weigh down, and his saggy face sags a little more. It is a sad, wise,
fanatical face, the mask of a man who has seen a great deal and
knows the worst.

– Robert Craft[1]

We went to a corner table and talked inconsequentially and it was
there, while I was yattering, that I noticed his eyes. They were pale
blue and depthless, with a curious icy light that made me think of
a creature who can see in the dark – the more so because they
were also the intimidating eyes of a blind man, with a hypnotist's
unblinking blue. His magic was in his eyes, but coldly blazing
they gave away nothing but this warning of indestructible
certainty. When he stared at me I felt it was no use confessing –
he knew my secrets.

– Paul Theroux[2]

In Paul Theroux's novel, *Picture Palace* (1978), the narrator, Maude
Pratt, who is a famous photographer, looks back over her life, recalling
particularly her incestuous passion for her brother and her encounters
with her camera subjects such as D.H. Lawrence (a randy old man),
Robert Frost (niggardly and mean-spirited beneath the folksy charm)
and Ernest Hemingway (graceful under pressure). What has particularly stimulated this recollection, however, is not simply the prospect
of a retrospective of her work but an encounter with Graham Greene,
whose photograph she has been commissioned to take. As the above
epigraph indicates, his physical presence is intimidating, particularly
the piercing blue eyes. Over dinner, Greene (in Theroux's knowing

narrative) makes reference to encounters with Castro, Truffaut, Jacqueline Bisset and Kim Philby, and also offers his theory of creativity which a reader would have been familiar with from *A Sort of Life* – namely, the virtue and cultivation of a poor memory, so that 'what you forget becomes the compost of the imagination'. In encouraging Maude Pratt to write, Greene says: 'The less you know the better. You have forgotten memories.'[3] It is a telling phrase because it catches the sense of how Greene's novels are often at the borderline – the dangerous edge, if you will – of inventiveness and fact, literature and biography. One might say that Greene's novels are the 'forgotten memories' of his life.[4]

Graham Greene died on 3 April 1991 at the Hopital de-la Providence at Vevey in Switzerland. Two of the closest companions of his later years, Yvonne Cloetta and Father Leopoldo Duran were in attendance at his death. His estranged wife, Vivien, to whom he had written a letter asking for forgiveness the year before, attended the funeral; and he was buried in Corseaux not far from the grave of his old friend, Charlie Chaplin. Later in the year on 6 June, a Memorial Requiem Mass was held in Westminster Cathedral. Those attending included members of the Greene family, Yvonne Cloetta, the publisher Max Reinhardt, Evelyn Waugh's son Auberon, ambassadors, or their representatives, from six different countries (Cuba, Nicaragua, Switzerland, Italy, Spain and Czechoslovakia), Sir Richard Attenborough and Harold Pinter.[5] Tributes were paid by his niece, Louise Dennys, Muriel Spark and Sir Alec Guinness. In his diary a few months after the event, Sir Alec was to remember the event and the speech of Dame Muriel Spark: 'In her tribute to Graham she spoke of the financial help he gave her when she was a struggling writer. She said, "It was typical of Graham that with the monthly cheques he often sent a few bottles of red wine to 'take the edge off cold charity'." It says something very pleasing about both of them.'[6]

At the time of his death, he had become one of the most honoured writers of the century. He had been made a Companion of Honour in 1966; and he held honorary doctorates at the Universities of Cambridge (1962), Edinburgh (1967), Oxford (1979) and Moscow (1988). Cedric Watts has enumerated other prizes won – the Shakespeare Prize (Hamburg, 1969), the John Dos Passos Prize (1980), the Jerusalem Prize (1980); made a Chevalier de la Legion d'Honneur and a Commandeur des Arts et Lettres in France in 1967 and 1984 respectively, and an Honorary Citizen of Anacapri in 1978; and awarded the Medal of the City of Madrid in 1980, the Grand Cross of Panama's Order of Vasco Nunez de Balboa in 1983, and Nicaragua's Order of Ruben Dario in 1987.[7] The only major honour that eluded him was the Nobel Prize for Literature, an honourable omission because, as Meyer (1989) pointed out, other eminently eligible writers who had also been overlooked since the inauguration of the prize in 1901 would have included Tolstoy, Ibsen, Zola, Chekhov, Strindberg, Hardy, Rilke, James, Conrad, Proust, Joyce and Virginia Woolf.[8] (Bryan Forbes has made a similar point from a reverse perspective: 'can anyone quickly name the last three recipients of the Nobel?'[9]) Nevertheless, Greene can undoubtedly claim to be one of the most famous non-recipients of the Nobel Prize, a fact nicely underlined by John Gielgud's writer-hero, raging against the dying of the light, in Alain Resnais's film, *Providence* (1977), scripted by David Mercer. '"Why haven't you got the Nobel Prize, daddy? Our English master says you aren't nearly as good as Graham Greene,"' he says at one stage in scornful imitation of his son, before adding with bilious relish: 'Well, sack the bugger, say I. Some of us, fart-face, wonder why Graham Greene hasn't won the Nobel Prize either!'

The point is worth dwelling on because, since his death, the status of Greene's literary reputation has become a matter of keen literary debate. With a tendency towards self-deprecation of his literary talents, Greene himself always felt he was one of the 'goods' rather than the 'greats' (he said so when interviewed for the 'Greene at 80' BBC Radio programme in 1984); and in a BBC 'Kaleidoscope' broadcast after his death, Malcolm Bradbury put him as 'the leader of the second rank' of major twentieth-century novelists, a judgment that enraged Bryan Forbes.[10] Like many artists, who have an ideal in their mind at the outset of what they are trying to achieve and are only conscious at the end of how far they have fallen short, Greene seemed more aware of failure in intent than success of execution. He would declare himself satisfied with scenes – the three-cornered love scene of *The Quiet American*, the chess game in *Our Man in Havana*, the Mrs Paterson in Boulogne chapters in *Travels With My Aunt* – more than complete novels, though he did tend to stick up for *England Made Me*, *Travels With My Aunt* and *The Honorary Consul* as his most underrated novels. At the time of his death, two of the most pondered critical assessments from his fellow novelists of different generations came from William Golding and Ian McEwan. 'Graham Greene was in a class by himself,' declared Golding, himself a Nobel Prize winner, of course, and a piercing observer of modern Fallen Man. 'He will be read and remembered as the ultimate chronicler of twentieth century man's consciousness and anxiety.'[11] In his obituary for *The Guardian* newspaper, Ian McEwan wrote: 'For me, and it must be true of all writers under fifty, he has been a lifetime companion. Some of the first grown-up books I read were by Graham Greene... One of the first lessons I took from them was that a serious novel could be an exciting novel – that the novel of adventure could also be the novel of ideas.'

McEwan's final formulation puts its finger on a key element of Greene's artistry and the controversy surrounding it. We have seen throughout this text how Greene's work – from 'Across the Bridge' and *The Power and the Glory* to *The Third Man* and *The Human Factor* – is often about the difficulty and tension of crossing borders; and how his characterisation similarly challenges conventional borderlines of behaviour and moral judgment – the charming villain, the noble sinner, the God-tormented killer, or, to borrow the Browning formulation Greene loved so much, 'the honest thief, the tender murderer, the superstitious atheist'. It seems therefore wholly appropriate that Greene as a writer should similarly be seen to straddle the border – between entertainer and artist, novelist of adventure and excitement co-existing with novelist of intellect and ideas. He is what, in classical music terms, would be called a 'crossover' artist, who has the gift of appealing both to the intelligentsia and the masses. Even as I write, this polarity is exemplified by, on the one hand, the appearance in recent weeks of a weighty and esoteric critical volume of over 600 pages and 1600 footnotes that deals with just one aspect of Greene's work (*Perceptions of Religious Faith in the Work of Graham Greene* – see bibliography); and, on the other, by the imminence of a new mainstream film of *The Quiet American* starring Michael Caine and Brendan Fraser that is clearly designed for a mass market. Something of this dichotomy of recognition is delightfully caught in Richard Kelly's recent film about an alienated teenager *Donnie Darko* (2002), when a member of the Parent Teachers Association objects to a novel of Greene's being on the English syllabus on account of its being a work of pornography. 'Do you even know who Graham

Greene is?' she is asked, to which she replies: 'Oh please, I think we've all seen *Bonanza*.'

It seems to me that the critical controversy over Greene can be particularly defined by what might be called Greene's quarrel with Modernism (or, to put it the other way round, the quarrel that advocates of Modernism have had with Greene). It is clear that, in a twentieth-century literary canon dominated by the esoteric, experimental genius of writers such as Joyce, Woolf, Yeats and Eliot, the relatively conventional narrative strategies of a Greene might seem a little conservative and technically unadventurous. (The same attitude tended to be taken towards the poetry of Thomas Hardy before the advocacy of people such as Philip Larkin and Donald Davie compelled a revision of attitudes.) It is clear that Greene was aware of the modernist tendencies of his contemporaries and the modernist preferences of the literary intelligentsia, but that, at a certain stage, he decided to go his own way. The novel that marks this turning point has always seemed to me to be *England Made Me*. It is his most experimental, overtly modernist novel, with a variety of advanced techniques that draw attention to the writing in a way that Greene was later to avoid. There is the muted use of Joycean stream-of-consciousness in the second section of Part One, when the hero Anthony's mind flicks formlessly, unchronologically across his past; and there is the evocation of Kate's dream-state when she is in bed with Krogh but dreaming of her father. At one stage, dialogue is crosscut across several conversations in the manner of Flaubert's *Madame Bovary* and Huxley's *Brave New World*. Rather like Joyce in the opening part of *A Portrait of the Artist as a Young Man*, Greene deploys the literary equivalent of a cinematic shock cut at the moment after Krogh has proposed marriage to Kate as a business arrangement and Kate's subliminal, almost subconscious anxiety is suggested by her sudden memory-flash of a tramcar out of control.[12] As with a modernist text like T.S. Eliot's *The Waste Land*, there are a lot of literary allusions that deepen the novel's texture – to Rupert Brooke, William Blake, Shakespeare's *Pericles* (with its motifs of incest and death by drowning that occur in the novel). Like much modernist literature, it is what one could call a poetic novel. Michael Shelden has shown how some of the lines in the novel can be laid out like an Imagist poem.[13] Indeed, the novel seems organised almost as much in relation to its imagery as in relation to its narrative. One of the pervasive images is that of dust; and the whole trajectory of the novel could be traced through the way Greene develops this image in relation to Anthony, Minty, and, by contrast, Kate (whose pet hate is dust on a mirror) and Krogh, who is all glass and steel, the internationalist present against England's richer, but anachronistic, dust. That kind of poetic organisation is characteristic of Modernist writing; and you will not find it deployed in quite the same way anywhere else in Greene's work.

Yet, Greene will not stick with that style and the final part of *England Made Me* drifts almost involuntarily into the realm of political thriller that will become a hallmark of his future fiction. It compels you to think of that conversation that Bendrix has with the literary critic Waterbury in *The End of the Affair*. ' "You used stream-of-consciousness in one of your books," Waterbury says. "Why did you abandon it?" ' To which Bendrix replies: 'Oh, I don't know. Why does one change a flat?'[14] Actually, I think by that time Greene knew very well why he had abandoned it. He had shown he could do it but it was not a method he felt happy with or expressed what he wanted to do. Moreover, he had aesthetic and ethical reservations about Modernism which were to become clearer as his career developed. They seem to me to centre on three main objections.

In that conversation in *The End of the Affair*, Waterbury tries to get Bendrix to comment on E.M. Forster but the novelist refuses to be drawn. Ironically, it was with Forster that Greene had his first quarrel with Modernism, notably to do with Forster's passage about 'The Story' in *Aspects of the Novel* (1927). 'Yes – oh dear yes – the novel tells a story,' Forster famously intoned. 'That is the fundamental aspect without which it could not exist. That is the highest factor common to all novels, and I wish that it was not so, that it could be something different – melody, or perception of the truth, not this low atavistic form.'[15] To play down the importance of narrative in favour of complex psychology or linguistic virtuosity was undoubtedly in the interests of the Modernist novelist who was not noted for the ability to provide a mesmerising plot (and I would include Forster in this: whatever other virtues he had, his plotting was often crude and unconvincing[16]). But Greene resented this. 'I'm a storyteller,' he insisted.[17] To Marie-Francois Allain, he said: 'I've always enjoyed telling stories, and my impression is that readers prefer this to the nouveau roman.'[18] One aspect of his distancing himself from the Modernists, then, was their disdain for an element of fiction which Greene both valued and at which he excelled.

A second reason for his quarrel with Modernism after the experimentation with *England Made Me* had more to do with the temper of the times. The urgency of the political situation in the 1930s seemed to demand of the writer a more socially committed role, not necessarily in terms of action but certainly in terms of writing about contemporary events. The more rarefied 'art for art's sake' stance of the Modernists (where a masterpiece was all that mattered), their turning aside from modern society in a kind of superior contempt, no longer seemed a relevant or adequate response: the world situation was deteriorating so drastically that soon there may not be any society left to feel superior to. (George Orwell writes about this artistic dilemma superbly in his essay 'Inside the Whale'.) An epic divertissement such as Joyce's *Finnegan's Wake* was a luxury writers could no longer afford: they had to add their voices against Fascism, their warning against complacency and indifference, their apprehensions for the future, as Greene will do, obliquely or directly, in *England Made Me, A Gun For Sale, Brighton Rock, Confidential Agent* and *The Ministry of Fear*.

However, the most important expression of his resistance to Modernism comes in an essay he wrote in 1945 on a writer he much admired, Francois Mauriac. For Greene, the immediate attraction of Mauriac has to do with his very traditionalism: 'he is a writer for whom the visible world has not ceased to exist, whose characters have the solidity and importance of men with souls to save or lose, and a writer who claims the traditional and essential right of a novelist to comment, to express his views'.[19] The essay begins with Greene's lament for what he calls the disappearance of the religious sense in the English novel after the death of Henry James in 1916. The novel had become purely subjective, he thought: it had lost sight of the physical world and characters existed only in their own senses and not in a larger world of God's making. In the following passage he seems to be quite specifically targeting for attack Virginia Woolf's ground-breaking essays 'Mr Bennett and Mrs Brown' and 'Modern Fiction' which had been taken as a blueprint of procedure by the Modernist novelist:

Mrs Dalloway walking down Regent Street was aware of the glitter of shop windows, the smooth passage of cars, the conversation of shoppers, but it was only a Regent Street seen by Mrs Dalloway that was conveyed to the reader: a charming whimsical rather sentimental prose poem was what Regent Street had become: a current of air, a touch of scent, a sparkle of glass. But, we protest, Regent Street too has a right to exist: it is more real than Mrs Dalloway, and we look back with nostalgia towards the chop houses, the mean courts, the still Sunday streets of Dickens. Dickens's characters were of immortal importance, and the houses in which they loved, the mews in which they damned themselves were lent importance by their presence. They were given the right to exist as they were, distorted, if at all, only by their observer's eye – not further distorted at a second remove by an imagined character.[20]

The creative artist in Greene cannot resist expressing his opposition to Woolf through a sly and wicked parody of her style. Also, as he says later: 'The exclusion of the author can go too far. Even the author, poor devil, has a right to exist' – a witty, percipient comment which, if heeded, might have saved some literary theorists years of anguish.[21] But the crux of the argument is clear: if Virginia Woolf attacked Arnold Bennett, along with John Galsworthy and H.G. Wells, for exaggerating the physical at the expense of the psychological, Greene's counter-attack was to suggest that Woolf and other Modernists went too far the other way, foregrounding the psychological at the expense of the physical.[22] They overemphasised individual consciousness and sensibility at the expense of the reality of the visible world – or, to put it in theological terms, at the expense of God's creation. When Greene at a certain point in *England Made Me* turns his back on literary experimentation and confronts the brutality of the modern political world, he is symbolically rejecting what he sees as the egocentricity and narcissism of Modernism and mapping out his future path and concerns as a novelist.

The consequences of this for his subsequent literary reputation were severe. To this day, it accounts for his underestimation and his neglect on campus courses in favour of the canonical giants of Modernism: the story-tellers and realists of his school are still regarded as arid, simplistic and old-fashioned. (Yet how many of his twentieth-century rivals have created such a distinctive physical, psychological and moral terrain as Greeneland?) But a second consequence was more positive. Consciously or not, Greene brought back into the modern novel the religious sense he felt the Modernists had removed. 'Here is life without God – just look at it!': that was George Orwell's summary of the spiritual atmosphere of Joyce's *Ulysses*. By contrast, the spiritual climate in Greene, particularly in a work like *The End of the Affair*, reminds one of Cranly's rebuke to Stephen Dedalus in the final part of *A Portrait of the Artist as a Young Man*: 'your mind is supersaturated with the religion in which you say you disbelieve'. In the fifteen years or so after *England Made Me*, Greene will write his own *Four Quartets*, that series of major religious novels (and how varied they are) on which, for many critics, the greatness of Greene as a writer can most powerfully be argued – *Brighton Rock*, *The Power and the Glory*, *The Heart of the Matter* and *The End of the Affair*.

Nevertheless, Greene's appeal and greatness go further than bringing God back into literature. His novels are in no sense an attempt at religious conversion. Indeed, like another great Catholic convert, Gustav Mahler,[23] his work thrives on doubt and despair and the search for, rather than the certainty of, ultimate meaning. From childhood, loyalty had always seemed a mixed blessing to Greene and his profession of the virtue of disloyalty could be applied to his own wayward Catholicism, which he needed, he said, 'to measure my evil against'.[24] What gives Greene his universality is his compassion for the individual in working out his or her own salvation, and the intensity with which his novels dramatise the infinite importance of an individual's moral actions.

In the latter part of his career, politics displaces religion at the forefront of his fiction. England made him, yet no other English novelist has such an international variety of settings in his global exposure of political horror and hypocrisy. As he traverses Europe, Liberia, Mexico, Africa, Vietnam, Cuba, Haiti, South America and elsewhere, Greene becomes a spectator of history and his novels sound the century as disturbingly and eloquently as the symphonies of Shostakovich. In his advocacy of democracy and humanity, he has the fearlessness of the truly free man that Rossellini recognised in Chaplin; and, in his exposure of injustice, like Chaplin he eschews narrow nationality in favour of citizenship of the world.

The Greene machine rolls on. In the last two years, we have had two remakes of film versions of his work (*The End of the Affair, The*

Quiet American) and these will undoubtedly continue, as film-makers, now less constrained by censorship considerations, attempt to get nearer in spirit and content to the originals. Bizarrely, there has been talk of musical versions: a long-mooted John Barry musical based on *Brighton Rock* (Greene at one time in the 1960s worked with Barry on a libretto); a musical version of Christopher Hawtree's anthology of Greene's letters to the press, *Yours Etc.*, starring Daniel Day-Lewis; and there is already Malcolm Williamson's operatic version of *Our Man in Havana*, which Greene liked. There will no doubt continue to be attempts to adapt his novels for the stage. Rather like his idol, Henry James, his novels seem to work better on stage than his own plays. (There have been outstanding theatrical productions in recent years of *Brighton Rock*, *The End of the Affair* and *Travels With My Aunt*.) There must surely – on grounds of curiosity alone – eventually be a public performance of his hitherto unproduced play, *A House of Reputation*.[25] Indeed, now that the aversion for the 'well-made play' has subsided and the formerly derided Terence Rattigan has been reclaimed on stage and film by such modern luminaries as Karel Reisz, Mike Figgis and David Mamet, it could be that Greene's plays, which have been neglected for years, are ripe for rediscovery. It is worth remembering that Kenneth Tynan called *The Living Room* 'the best first play of its generation'; that *The Complaisant Lover* is one of the most scintillating sex comedies of its time; and that the plays themselves attracted actors of the calibre of Dorothy Tutin, Eric Portman, Irene Worth, John Gielgud, Ralph Richardson, Phyllis Calvert and Paul Scofield.

'I sometimes feel I am more than a hundred years old,' said Greene on his eightieth birthday. It has been an extraordinary pilgrimage – artistically, personally, theologically, politically. Finally how to sum it up? Let Greene himself have the last word on his world in that wonderful description in *The Power and the Glory* (Part 2, Chapter 3) when the priest has been captured and is languishing in prison and reflecting on his situation:

> It was like the end. There was no need to hope any longer. The ten years' hunt was over at last. There was silence all around him. This place was very like the world: overcrowded with lust and crime and unhappy love, it stank to heaven: but he realised that it

was possible to find peace there, when you knew for certain that the time was short.

It would be pleasant to think that Greene himself in the end had found peace amidst the stench of humanity that he had anatomised so wisely, and which 'stank *to heaven*' [my italics]. On Greene the craftsman, perhaps the final word might go to Keith Waterhouse (Greene would have liked to go out with a joke) as he reflected on the saga of *The Tenth Man*, the tale that Greene could not remember having written. 'Greene seems unable to put pen to paper without writing like Graham Greene,' wrote Waterhouse (*The Times*, 6 September 1984), adding incredulously, 'and then forgetting about it'. Pondering that for a moment, he concludes ruefully: 'What hope is there for the rest of us?'

Notes

Introduction: secret sharer

1. Graham Greene, *British Dramatists*, London: Collins, 1942, p. 16.
2. John Le Carré, *The Spy Who Came in from the Cold*, London: Victor Gollancz, 1963, p. 140.
3. Ford Madox Ford, *The Good Soldier* (1915), London: Penguin English Library, 1964, p. 122.
4. Donald Rayfield, *Anton Chekhov: A Life*, London: HarperCollins, 1997, p. 315.
5. This image was particularly popularised after the publication of *The End of the Affair* and through Kenneth Tynan's profile of Greene in an issue of *Harper's Bazaar* (February 1953). 'Graham Greene has never been able to build up a resistance to sin,' Tynan wrote. '... He looks retiringly pedantic, and sits hunched, with hands and knees crossed, peering out at the grey flux of circumstance with bright, moist, hopeless eyes ... A man, you might suppose, who feels he has disappointed life as much as life has disappointed him: the impression he leaves, as he wanders rangily off along a crowded street, is one of acute solitariness.' See *Profiles*, London: Nick Hern Books, 1989, pp. 51–7.
6. See John Atkins, *Graham Greene*, London: Calder & Boyars, 1957, p. 78.
7. See *The Pleasure Dome*, London: Secker & Warburg, 1972, pp. 144–5.
8. Tynan, p. 52.
9. *A Sort of Life*, London: Bodley Head, 1971, p. 127.
10. There is a useful chapter on the meaning of 'Greeneland' in Cedric Watts's admirable introduction to the author, *A Preface to Greene*, London: Pearson Education Ltd, 1997, pp. 142–8. The origins of the term are generally attributed to a reference to 'Greenland' in a song Ann sings in Chapter 3 of *A Gun for Sale*; and to Arthur Calder-Marshall's early essay on Greene in *Horizon* (May 1940) in which he talks of a territory called Greeneland that is characterised by seediness. Greene himself disliked the term, thinking it gave the impression of a private world of his own imagining when his novels were actually inspired by an external and perceptible reality.

Why do I write?

1. *Why Do I Write?: An Exchange of Views between Elizabeth Bowen, Graham Greene and V.S. Pritchett*, London: Percival Marshall & Co. Ltd, 1948, p. 48.

2. *Joseph Andrews* (Book 1, Chapter 1). Fielding is referring to *An Apology for the Life of Mr Colley Cibber, Comedian,* first published in 1740. Greene would have known this passage as he had written about Fielding in his essay 'Fielding and Sterne' in 1937. The 'Kolly Kibber' business in *Brighton Rock* could well have been indirectly suggested by this reference.
3. See *Graham Greene: Yours Etc., Letters to the Press, 1945–89,* edited and introduced by Christopher Hawtree, London: Reinhardt Books, 1989. As Hawtree says: 'The strength of the fiction – the art of the matter – is in its allying observation and imagination, a continual awareness of technique, one part of which is transcription: although it uses much the same words, how different in effect is "A Memory of Indo–China" (*Listener,* 15 September 1955) from the vertical raid which forms a part of the complex time-scheme and narrative method of *The Quiet American.*' (p. xii)
4. *A Sort of Life,* London: Bodley Head, 1971, p. 182.
5. See Henry James, *The Art of the Novel,* with an introduction by R.P. Blackmur. New York: Charles Scribner's Sons, 1962, pp. 119–39. The preface was first published in 1908.
6. 'Foreword', *Pavilions by the Sea: The Memoirs of a Hotel-Keeper,* by Tom Laughton, London: Chatto & Windus, 1977, p. ix.
7. See Lillian Hellman's *Pentimento,* London: Quartet Books, 1976, p. 205. The advice might seem basic but Hellman notes that 'the next day after Edmund said it, I went to work on *Toys in the Attic.*'
8. See Simon Callow's *Orson Welles: The Road to Xanadu,* London: Jonathan Cape, 1995, p. ix.
9. *Why Do I Write?,* pp. 30–1. The virtue of disloyalty will also be elaborated in his short story 'Under The Garden' from the collection *A Sense of Reality* (1963). At one stage Javett tells the narrator: 'Be disloyal. It's your duty to the human race. The human race needs to survive and it's the loyal man who dies first from anxiety or a bullet or overwork. If you have to earn a living, boy, and the price they make you pay is loyalty, be a double agent – and never let either of the two sides know your real name. The same applies to women and God.' (*Collected Short Stories,* London: Penguin, 1986, p. 202)
10. *Why Do I Write?,* p. 32. The reference is to Robert Browning's poem 'Bishop Blougram's Apology'. In *A Sort of Life,* Greene famously quoted some lines from the poem that he said could stand as an epigraph to all his novels:

> Our interest's on the dangerous edge of things.
> The honest thief, the tender murderer,
> The superstitious atheist, demi-rep
> That loves and saves her soul in new French books –
> We watch while these in equilibrium keep
> The giddy line midway. (ll. 396–400)

Greene quotes the poem again in *Ways of Escape* (p. 196) when he is recalling his argument with Evelyn Waugh over *A Burnt-Out Case* and answering the latter's criticism that the novel could be taken as a recantation of faith:

> What we have gained then by our unbelief
> Is a life of doubt diversified by faith,
> For one of faith diversified by doubt:
> We called the chessboard white, – we call it black. (ll. 210–13)

In the BBC's *Arena* programme, Greene's definition of the storyteller's task – 'to elicit sympathy and a measure of understanding for those who lie outside the boundaries of state approval' – was also recalled. Interestingly, at a symposium during the annual Graham Greene Festival in Berkhamsted in 2000, the film producer Stephen Woolley, who had produced the remake of *The End of the Affair* (1999) with director Neil Jordan, described the heroes in Jordan's films in very Greene-like terms: 'characters in a twilight world and at the fringes of society'. It might explain why Jordan would seem such a natural director of Greene's work: their main characters occupy a similarly dark and treacherous moral terrain.

11. George Orwell, *Why I Write* (1947). See Orwell, *Collected Essays*, London: Secker & Warburg, 1961, p. 435.

12. Quoted by Greene in his 1939 essay 'Man Made Angry', in *Collected Essays*, London: Penguin edition, 1970, p. 104. Greene would have known too of that splendid moment in Samuel Butler's *The Way of all Flesh* (1884) when the narrator Overton warns all teachers to beware of the fact that the boy you are currently tormenting might be the one person who is going to take revenge by recording his experience in a book. 'Never see a wretched little heavy-eyed mite sitting on the edge of a chair against your study wall without saying to yourselves, "perhaps this boy is he who, if I am not careful, will one day tell the world what manner of man I was".' (End of Chapter 28.) Published 1903, and here quoted from the 1966 Penguin English Library edition, p. 148.

13. Edmund Bergler, *The Writer and Psychoanalysis*, New York: Doubleday, 1954, p. 236.

14. Introduction, *The Viper of Milan*, by Marjorie Bowen. London: Penguin Books, 1963, p. 9.

15. Norman Sherry has pointed out that this was not the case. Lionel Carter was still alive and lived until 1971, the year of *A Sort of Life*.

16. *A Sort of Life*, p. 82.

17. Ibid., p. 63.

18. *Ways of Escape*, p. 211. In the same passage he wonders how those who do not have this kind of outlet, who do not write, compose or paint, can manage to escape this madness: what kind of resources do they have access to?

19. In *A Sort of Life* (p. 90), Greene mentions that his grandfathers on both sides of the family were depressives. He did not know of the existence of

his maternal grandfather (who had lived until 1924, when Greene was twenty) until coming across a footnote reference to him when reading Swinburne's letters. According to Greene, this grandfather, while an undergraduate at Trinity College, Cambridge had been part-author of a favourable review of the notorious first volume of *Poems and Ballads* (1866) and Swinburne had asked to see it. As a sort of private joke, there is a comical reference to Swinburne's name in *The Confidential Agent*.

20. Henry James, 'The Art of Fiction' (1884), published in *Henry James: Selected Literary Criticism*, edited by Morris Shapira, London: Peregrine Books, 1968, p. 86.
21. *A Sort of Life*, p. 185.
22. The symbol of the teddy bear might have had some resonance for Greene. In his controversial biography, *Graham Greene: The Enemy Within* (New York: Random House, 1994, pp. 59–60), Michael Shelden makes a big play of the fact that Greene himself well into his adult life had a teddy bear called Ted of whom he seemed exceptionally fond. A teddy bear similarly has an important role to play in Greene's early story of 1935, *The Bear Fell Tree*: it is the hero's good luck charm that, after his death in a plane crash, falls into the hands of his evil friend called (inevitably) Carter. Shelden sees Greene's toy bear as an important symbol for him of 'what he had lost in his teens – a sense of innocence, a feeling of security'.

The books in my life

1. *A Sort of Life*, pp. 52–3. Henry Pullen, the narrator of *Travels With My Aunt* (Part 2, Chapter 3) makes a similar observation: 'One's life is more formed, I sometimes think, by books than by human beings; it is out of books one learns about love and pain at second hand.' It is his way of explaining his passionless nature, which he blames on his father's library: there is not much unbridled eroticism in Walter Scott.
2. Anthony Mockler, *Graham Greene: Three Lives*, Arbroath: Hunter Mackay, 1994, p. 7.
3. See *The Annotated Library of Graham Greene*, London: Rampant Lions Press, 1993. Catalogued by Jean McNeil and Nicholas Dennys. Foreword by William Trevor.
4. *Greene on Capri: A Memoir*, London: Virago Press, 2000, p. 66.
5. There are good accounts of Greene's experience as a publisher in W.J. West's *The Quest for Graham Greene*, London: Weidenfeld & Nicholson, 1997, pp. 115–20; and in Norman Sherry's *The Life of Graham Greene, Volume Two*, London: Penguin edition, 1995, pp. 187–204.
6. *Ways of Escape*, p. 15.
7. *A Sort of Life*, p. 208. Anthony Mockler challenges this in his book on Greene, claiming that Greene did re-read *Heart of Darkness* later than he said and that he exaggerated (or at least misremembered) the hostility of Frank Swinnerton's review (pp. 66–7).

8. Cedric Watts, *A Preface to Greene*, Harlow: Pearson Education Limited, 1997, pp. 124–5.
9. David Lodge, *The Art of Fiction*, London: Penguin Books, 1997, pp. 159–60.
10. Alec Guinness, *A Positively Final Appearance*, London: Hamish Hamilton,1999, p. 186.
11. *A Sort of Life*, p. 114.
12. Ibid., p. 115.
13. Samuel Hynes, *The Auden Generation*, London: Faber & Faber, 1976, p. 234.
14. Valentine Cunningham, *British Writers of the Thirties*, Oxford: Oxford University Press, 1989, p. 20. It might be worth noting here that the reference is specifically to Greene's review of Lewis Milestone's film, *Anything Goes*, and the 'really dreadful woman singer' referred to is the sublimely strident Ethel Merman – admittedly, the last performer to whom one would attach the epithet 'Audenesque'.
15. M.D. Zabel, 'Graham Greene' in *Forms of Modern Fiction*, edited by William Van O'Connor, Minnesota: University of Minnesota Press, 1948, p. 273. The phrase 'our baseless optimism that is so much more appalling than our despair' is used by Greene to conclude his 1938 short story 'Across the Bridge'.
16. Richard Hoggart, *Auden: An Introductory Essay*, London: Chatto & Windus, 1951, pp. 48–50.
17. *The Heart of the Matter*, London: Penguin, revised edition, 1978, p. 186.
18. Ibid., p. 55.
19. *The Honorary Consul*, London: Bodley Head, 1973, p. 252.
20. Hoggart, p. 50. It could be argued that the effect tends to be more mental or intellectual than visual. Interestingly, for a writer who has often been praised for his ability to evoke place, Greene held the view that 'I have very little visual imagination.' 'Introduction', *In Search of A Character*, London: Bodley Head, 1961, p. 9.
21. *Collected Essays*, London: Bodley Head, 1969, p. 13.
22. Ibid., p. 16.
23. *Greene on Capri: A Memoir*, p. 29.
24. 'Introductory Note', *The Viper of Milan*, 1906: London: Peacock Books, 1963, p. 9.
25. *The Lost Childhood*, p. 17.
26. Ibid., p. 17.

The Greene routine

1. Quoted by Greene at the end of his essay 'Fielding and Sterne' from *From Anne to Victoria*, edited by Bonamy Dobree, London: Cassell & Co., 1937, p. 289.
2. *London Mercury*, October 1935, pp. 562–5.
3. See Steven Soderbergh's *Getting Away With It*, Faber & Faber, 1999, p. 198.

4. Ken Annakin, *So You Wanna Be A Director?*, Sheffield: Tomahawk Press, 2001, p. 149.
5. *Ways of Escape*, pp. 68–9. Such are the mysteries of creative composition. One is reminded of the story of Sir Walter Scott who wrote *The Bride of Lammermoor* under the influence of laudanum to kill the pain in his legs and apparently could not remember a thing about the experience. When the publisher sent him the proofs to correct, he did not recognise it as his own work.
6. 'Preface', *The Third Man* and *The Fallen Idol*, London: Heinemann, 1950, p. 9. The sentence was: 'I had paid my last respects to Harry a week ago, when his coffin was lowered into the frozen February ground, so that it was with incredulity that I saw him pass by, without a sign of recognition, amongst the host of strangers in the Strand.'
7. See 'Introduction' in *In Search of a Character* (London: Bodley Head, 1961, p. 9) where Greene says: 'when five years later I began to write *The Heart of the Matter* I regretted my lack of notes. So many small details of life in Freetown had sunk for ever into the unconscious. I had stayed too long, so that I took too much for granted, for I have very little visual imagination and only a short memory.'
8. Bryan Forbes, *A Divided Life*, London: Heinemann, 1992, p. 214. It was W.B. Yeats who most pointedly expressed the creative effort involved in appearing effortless in his poem 'Adam's Curse' (1904):

> I said 'a line will take us hours maybe
> Yet if it does not seem a moment's thought
> Our stitching and unstitching has been naught.'

9. Michael Meyer, *Not Prince Hamlet: Literary and Theatrical Memoirs*, London: Secker & Warburg, 1989, p. 206.
10. *A Sort of Life*, p. 181.
11. Ibid., p. 141.
12. Leopoldo Duran, *Graham Greene: Friend and Brother*, London: HarperCollins, 1994, p. 206.
13. Ibid., p. 210.
14. See *Ways of Escape*, p. 30. The other characters he mentions of this type are the barmaid in *Brighton Rock*, Wilson in *The Heart of the Matter*, Smythe in *The End of the Affair*, and the journalist Parkinson in *A Burnt-Out Case*.
15. *A Sort of Life*, p. 202.
16. See Greene's introduction to *The Pleasure-Dome: The collected film criticism 1935–40*, London: Secker & Warburg, 1972, pp. 3–4.
17. *Ways of Escape*, pp. 105–6.
18. *A Divided Life*, p. 213.
19. Duran, p. 288.
20. I am thinking of his open letter to Chaplin when the latter was being refused re-entry to America during the McCarthyist witch-hunt of Hollywood liberals (*New Statesman*, 27 September 1952). Greene mentions that

he suggested to Chaplin a scenario where the tramp appears before the House of UnAmerican Activities and has to explain to them the meaning of his most famous comedy routines while the Committee takes notes. Although Chaplin laughed off the suggestion, one can certainly see traces of it in *A King in New York*, with its banished hero in exile and its evocation of the atmosphere of spying and persecution in a McCarthyist America, in which the young son of an American communist (sensitively played by Chaplin's own son, Michael) is compelled to 'name names' to save his parents from prison.
21. *A Divided Life*, p. 218.

Greene on the screen

1. Marie-Francoise Allain, *The Other Man: Conversations with Graham Greene*, London: Bodley Head, 1982, pp. 132–3.
2. *A Sort of Life*, p. 11.
3. Quoted in David Parkinson's *Mornings in the Dark: The Graham Greene Film Reader*, London: Penguin Books, 1995, p. 385.
4. See Norman Sherry, *The Life of Graham Greene: Volume One 1904–1939*, London: Jonathan Cape, 1989, p. 244.
5. 'Introduction', *The Pleasure Dome: The collected film criticism 1935–40*, London: Secker & Warburg, 1972, p. 1.
6. See Parkinson, p. xvi.
7. Ibid., p. 388.
8. *The Pleasure Dome*, p. 1.
9. Orwell wrote, as follows, about his film reviewing experience: 'Everyone in this world has someone he can look down on, and I must say, from experience of both trades, that the book reviewer is better off than the film critic, who cannot even do his work at home, but has to attend trade shows at eleven in the morning and, with one or two exceptions, is expected to sell his honour for a glass of inferior sherry.' (George Orwell, *Collected Essays Volume 4*, London: Penguin, 1970, p. 218) I discuss Orwell's film criticism and his connections with the cinema in the chapter 'Age of Doublethink: George Orwell and the Cinema' in my book, *Filming Literature: the Art of Screen Adaptation*, London: Croom Helm, 1986, pp. 55–69. Orwell's interest in the cinema was more social than aesthetic. He had a great admiration for Chaplin's *The Great Dictator* (1940), which, I have argued, had a big influence on *Animal Farm* and *1984*.
10. First published in 1937 by Jonathan Cape and without a great deal of success (Cooke recalls being told by C.A. Lejeune that an earnest schoolboy had requested it in 1938 as a school prize 'if any copies could still be found'), the anthology was republished in 1971 and, for someone of my generation, was probably the first sight we had seen of Greene's film criticism. It precipitated the publication of the collected cinema writings of Greene, *The Pleasure Dome* the following year by the same publisher.

11. Dilys Powell, 'Graham Greene at 75', *The Listener*, 4 October 1979. Quoted in Parkinson, pp. ix–xx.
12. *The Spectator*, 7 August 1936. See *The Pleasure Dome*, p. 92.
13. *Night and Day*, 7 October 1937. See *The Pleasure Dome*, p. 173.
14. See Parkinson, pp. xxvii–xxviii.
15. Ibid., p. 406.
16. Robin Wood, *Hitchcock's Films*, London: Zwemmer, 1965, p. 13.
17. Quoted in Judith Adamson's 'Graham Greene as film critic', *Sight and Sound*, Spring 1972, p. 106.
18. Peter Conrad, *The Hitchcock Murders*, London: Faber & Faber, 2000, p. 212.
19. *The Spectator*, 19 July 1935. Quoted in *The Pleasure Dome*, p. 10.
20. *Night and Day*, 9 December 1937.
21. As a response to the style, Reed's friend, the great Hollywood director William Wyler sent him a spirit level, with a note saying: 'Carol, next time you make a picture, just put it on the top of the camera, will you?' See Nicholas Wapshott's *The Man Between: A Biography of Carol Reed*, London: Chatto & Windus, 1990, p. 228.
22. Graham Greene, 'Subjects and Stories' in *Footnotes to the Film*, edited by Charles Davy, London: Lovat-Dickson, 1937, p. 66.
23. Ibid., pp. 67–8.
24. Ibid., p. 57.
25. Review, '*Modern Times*', *The Spectator*, 14 February 1936. Kenneth Allott is rather dismissive of that comparison, but it is surely conscious and deeply felt in Greene, even to the extent of deliberately evoking Conrad's own phrases when he describes the themes at the heart of his work: 'Those who read me know my conviction that the world, the temporal world, rests on a few very simple ideas; so simple that they must be as old as the hills. It rests notably, among others, on the idea of Fidelity.' (From *A Personal Record*. Quoted in Jocelyn Baines's *Joseph Conrad: A Critical Biography*, London: Weidenfeld Goldbacks, 1969, p. 450.)
26. The films that are usually grouped under this heading include the afore-mentioned films of Duvivier, Jean Renoir's *La Bête Humaine* (1938) and particularly the collaborations between director Marcel Carné and writer Jacques Prévert, *Quai des Brumes* (1938) and *Le Jour se Léve* (1940), often starring a doom-laden Jean Gabin. Although dubious of the usefulness and applicability of the term, Julian Petley has supplied a handy definition: 'If it means anything at all, this seems to imply a use of downbeat locations or sets, and a pessimistic view of man's destiny (realism), allied to shadowy, non-naturalistic photography and a constant desire on the part of the characters to escape their milieu and destiny (poetry).' (*BFI Distribution Library Catalogue 1978*, p. 162). For a definitive British film in this vein, one need look no further than *Odd Man Out* (1947), the first post-war film of Greene's finest cinematic collaborator, Carol Reed.
27. *Ways of Escape*, p. 18.
28. *A Sort of Life*, p. 199.
29. Ibid., p. 198.

30. Ibid., p. 199.
31. *Ways of Escape*, p. 200.
32. I am indebted to Philip French for drawing my attention to this particular passage.
33. *The Pleasure Dome*, p. 72. In the play, the accusation is one of lesbianism, which has been toned down for the 1936 film. (At this time and for many years after, the play was banned from the London stage.) William Wyler was to remake the film, magnificently, in 1961 as *The Children's Hour* (though called *The Loudest Whisper* in Great Britain), with Audrey Hepburn and Shirley MacLaine in the leading roles and the lesbian theme now explicit.
34. The precise quote from Picasso goes as follows: 'We all know that Art is not truth. Art is a lie that makes us realise truth.' (See Dore Ashton's *Picasso on Art*, 1972.) My acquaintance with this quotation came initially from its brilliant deployment to fool an audience in the Orson Welles film, *F for Fake* (1976), his delicious cinematic essay on forgery, magic and art and the connection between them. How appropriate that Welles should have some of his greatest film moments when playing Greene's most charming and chilling charlatan, Harry Lime, in *The Third Man*.
35. Michael Shelden, *Graham Greene: The Enemy Within*, London: Heinemann, 1994, p. 180. He notes how Alexander Korda had bought the screen rights for *The Power and the Glory* for £2000 before selling them to John Ford. 'After the war Korda paid £3000 for Greene's work on *The Fallen Idol*; £4000 for the rights to *The Heart of the Matter*; and £9000 for *The Third Man*. This last figure included the cost of a small yacht – the *Nausikaa* – which Greene used only briefly, and also the cost of buying the Villa Rosaio in Anacapri.'
36. *The Pleasure Dome*, p. 4.
37. Greene's involvement in this project is mentioned in *Yours Etc.* (p. 108) It seems to have been one of the first ideas he promoted when he left Heinemann publishers to become a director for the Bodley Head. In *The Quest for Graham Greene* (London: Weidenfeld & Nicholson, 1997), W.J. West elaborates interestingly on this and suggests that, in places, Chaplin's *My Autobiography* shows the imprint of Greene's advice. 'There are several places in the book where Greene's presence can almost be felt,' West writes. 'Chaplin had visited Hong Kong and had been introduced to a young priest from Connecticut who had been working in a leper colony for five years. When they came to part Chaplin shook his hand and, noticing it felt rough, turned it over and looked at it. "There were cracks and crevices and in the centre a white spot. 'That's not leprosy, I hope,' I said jokingly. He grinned and shook his head. A year later we heard he had died of it." Had Chaplin not had for a publisher the author of *A Burnt-Out Case*, this brief sketch might never have appeared' (pp. 184–5).
38. The story of how Greene came to land that part is told in *Mornings in the Dark*, p. 721. Apparently Truffaut did not know the identity of his new actor until after the scene had been shot and, although he usually

disliked practical jokes, was delighted by the deception. Curiously, there is a very Greene-like touch in the screenplay when the actress (Jacqueline Bissett) confides intimate details of her private life to her seemingly sympathetic director (Truffaut) and then is appalled to find that he has transferred some of her words directly to the character she plays in the film! 'There is a splinter of ice in the heart of every writer,' Greene famously wrote when describing how novelists will observe and feed on human misery simply for the acquisition of material useful to their work. Truffaut is suggesting that film directors behave similarly.

39. Famously, Sten had the same effect on Samuel Goldwyn who brought her over to Hollywood and, in one of his rare miscalculations of public taste, invested an enormous amount of time and money in an unsuccessful attempt to make her a star.

Laughter in the shadow of the gallows

1. *The Times*, 20 January 1983.
2. Michael Shelden, p. 308.
3. *Ways of Escape*, Penguin edition, 1981, p. 211.
4. When reviewing *The Heart of the Matter* for *The New Statesman*, Sackville-West usefully explained for the benefit of the non-Catholic reader the appalling implications of suicide for a Catholic: 'To the non-Catholic it must seem that there are many worse – less pardonable – sins: relentless cruelty, for instance, and treachery, and meanness. To which the Church replies that whereas cruelty and treachery can be wiped out by repentance ... the wretch who takes his own life has no time in which to repent of his sin. Suicide is unpardonable, quite as much because it is final, as because it is the goal of despair, than which no insult to God can be more profound.' Quoted in Sherry, Volume 2, p. 294.
5. *Graham Greene Newsletter*, Late Spring 2002, p. 7.
6. *The Other Man: Conversations with Graham Greene*, London: Bodley Head, 1983, p. 142.
7. *Ways of Escape*, p. 198.
8. *The Confidential Agent*, Penguin, 1963, pp. 136–7.
9. See Maria Couto's *Graham Greene: On the Frontier*, London: Macmillan, 1988, pp. 228–9. It should in fairness be noted that the cultural difference can cut both ways and that George Bernard Shaw's famous observation that England and America were divided by a common language could be applied to Greene. In *Mornings in the Dark*, David Parkinson provides a striking example of this when he notes that Greene's review of Lloyd Bacon's superb gangster movie, *Marked Woman* (1937) is premised on a misheard line of dialogue. Greene thought the line was 'It's feudal', which triggers learned allusions in the review to the *Anglo-Saxon Chronicle*: in fact, the line is 'It's futile', spoken in an American voice (see pp. 220, 718).
10. Preface, *The Third Man* and *The Fallen Idol*, London: Penguin, 1971, p. 11.
11. Michael Korda, *Charmed Lives*, London: Penguin, 1980, p. 218.

12. Joseph Conrad, *Heart of Darkness* (1902), New York: Bantam edition, 1962, p. 85.
13. Greene was puzzled by the reference to himself as a 'torturer' in the attack on him, inspired by Papa Doc, in *Graham Greene Unmasked*, launched after the publication of *The Comedians*. From Papa Doc, he thought, the description of 'torturer' might be construed as a compliment. But maybe they were thinking of his practical jokes.
14. Norman Sherry has observed that, in his lifetime, Greene travelled further than Marco Polo and that, in terms of travel, he may have spent more time in the air than on the ground.
15. The part was played on the London stage by Ralph Richardson, who was always alert to Greene's sense of the absurd. This is particularly evident in his marvellous comic performance as the Chief of the British Secret Service in the film of *Our Man in Havana*, utterly convinced that Wormold's sketches of the inside of a vacuum cleaner are evidence of the enemy's new nuclear capability.
16. According to *A Sort of Life*, Greene's hostility to dentists dates from childhood and a visit that left him 'rolling on the drawing-room floor in agony from an exposed nerve.' (pp. 35–6) It even infects his film reviewing. 'The new star, Miss Louise Campbell,' he wrote of the William Wellman film, *Men With Wings* (1938), 'was formerly a dental assistant, but none of the painful scenes at which she then assisted ever lasted two hours.' (*The Spectator*, 18 November 1938). Quoted in *Mornings in the Dark*, p. 273.
17. Kenneth Tynan, *Curtains*, London: Longmans, 1961, pp. 231–2.
18. I am thinking of the observation by Greene's narrator, Brown, when he says: 'Life was a comedy, not the tragedy for which I had been prepared, and it seemed to me that we were all... driven by an authoritative practical joker towards the extreme point of comedy' (*The Comedians*, London: Bodley Head, 1966, p. 34). The authoritative practical joker is God. The nature of the Universe and the human situation might all be attributable to the wicked sense of humour of its Creator.
19. See Michael Shelden, p. 352. He quotes, Michael Meyer, who had introduced Greene to Anita Bjork and who suggested that this incident in *The Complaisant Lover* had offended the sensibilities of Sweden's close-knit literary community, and particularly Dr Artur Lundkvist who dominated the Nobel literary committee.
20. Interestingly, Tom Stoppard was to use the line as the title of one of his radio plays, *The Dog It Was That Died* (1982), which, like *Our Man in Havana*, is a comedy about espionage. Stoppard, it will be remembered, wrote the screenplay for the film version of Greene's *The Human Factor*.
21. *Our Man in Havana*, p. 131.
22. The Ealing connection is particularly seen through the film, *Went the Day Well?* (1942), directed by Albert Cavalcanti and based on Greene's short story, 'The Lieutenant Died Last'. The film is consistently underrated in Quentin Falk's otherwise excellent *Travels in Greeneland* and there is no indication that Greene ever saw it. Yet, when he first thought of the idea

of a satire on the Secret Service, it was Cavalcanti with whom he discussed it.

23. Hitchcock was not offering enough money, apparently, and Greene anyway did not think it could survive his touch. Ironically, Hitchcock went on to make *North By North-West* (1959), one of his greatest films, which has much in common with *Our Man in Havana*. See Chapter 8 for a fuller discussion of this.

24. *A Sort of Life*, p. 71.

25. *The Other Man*, pp. 22–3. This is interesting because elsewhere Greene tended to be critical of readers who made a too easy identification between a character and his creator. It does suggest that this novel is different in this respect: that Greene's identification with his hero, Querry is unusually strong.

26. Images of leprosy proliferate in Greene, well in advance of *A Burnt-Out Case*, and may well derive, as W.J. West has persuasively argued, from his fascination with the nineteenth-century priest Father Damien, who had died of leprosy amongst the lepers he had been ministering to and whose courage and nobility were passionately defended in a famous open letter to *The Times* written by Robert Louis Stevenson. The image occurs in *Lord Rochester's Monkey*, p. 214; in *England Made Me*, where Anthony's untrustworthy smile is likened to a leper's bell; in *The Quiet American*, where innocence is likened to 'a dumb leper who has lost his bell, wandering the world meaning no harm'; and even in *The End of the Affair* where Sarah muses 'if I could love a leper's sores, could I love the boringness of Henry?'. It is curious too that a film with which Greene was tangentially involved around the time of researching *A Burnt-Out Case*, namely, *Ben-Hur* (1959) has a powerful and pervasive leper motif.

27. *Ways of Escape*, p. 230.

28. *A Burnt-Out Case*, Penguin edition, 1963, pp. 162–4.

29. Ibid., pp. 201–2.

30. Ibid., p. 15.

31. Ibid., p. 61.

32. Ibid., p. 191.

33. Ibid., p. 199.

34. Ibid., p. 199.

35. Greene always chose the names of his characters carefully, and I wonder whether the name is a deliberate allusion to George Stevens' great film, *Shane* (1953). There is even a storm during this scene, as in the film. Curiously, there is another allusion to *Shane* in *The Complaisant Lover* where a boy's offstage calls of 'Mother...' will remind her of her domestic responsibilities in a situation of emotional danger: a similar scene occurs in Stevens' film.

36. *A Burnt-Out Case*, pp. 202–5.

37. *The Guardian Weekend*, 31 October 1992, p. 10.

38. *Collected Short Stories*, Penguin, 1986, p. 194.

39. *The Other Man*, p. 129.

40. *Ways of Escape*, p. 210.
41. 'Introduction': *Author's Choice: Four Novels of Graham Greene*, Penguin, 1985, p. 7.
42. This is indicated by the novel's dedication, the significance of which is explained more fully in Chapter 6.
43. *A Burnt-Out Case*, p. 122.
44. *Ways of Escape*, p. 237.

A sort of autobiography: epigraphs and dedications

1. *Why The Epigraph?*, London: Nonesuch, 1989, pp. 7–8.
2. BBC *Arena*, Part 3, January 1993.
3. *A Sort of Life*, p. 73.
4. See Kenneth R. Morefield, 'A Catholic Writer Demands a Catholic Reading: Graham Greene's Use of Epitexts' in *Perceptions of Religious Faith in the Work of Graham Greene*, edited by Wm. Thomas Hill, Berne: Peter Lang, 2002, pp. 153–73.
5. *Why The Epigraph?*, p. 14.
6. Ibid., p. 8.
7. See Gary O'Connor, *Ralph Richardson*, London: Hodder & Stoughton, 1982, p. 250. O'Connor quotes the critic J.W. Lambert as saying that 'Richardson made him a Michelangelo, Greene made him a great ass.' Although Richardson had given supremely skilful performances in screen roles for Greene in *The Fallen Idol* and *Our Man in Havana* and, by most accounts, also on stage in *The Complaisant Lover*, the two fell out violently over *Carving A Statue*. Greene sent Richardson an angry letter about his performance which the actor, with due appropriateness, filed inside the cover of an illustrated book on Henry Moore's sculptures. The rift ran so deep that, in *A World of My Own*, Greene can still recall having hostile dreams about Richardson.
8. The precise phrase is not used by Wordsworth but is in a passage from Book 1 of *The Prelude*, when the poet is talking of 'Ye Presences of Nature' who employed 'such ministry' and who evoked in the young Wordsworth feelings of 'triumph, and delight, and hope, and fear' (see lines, 464–75).
9. Bryan Forbes, *A Divided Life*, London: Heinemann, 1992, p. 69.
10. *A Sort of Life*, p. 16.
11. From Judith Adamson's conference paper, 'The Long Wait for Aunt Augusta: Reflections on Graham Greene's Fictional Women', presented at The Graham Greene Literary Festival, Berkhamsted, October 2001.
12. See Alex Kershaw's 'An end of the affairs', *The Guardian Weekend*, 31 October 1992, p. 7.
13. See *The Guardian*, 25 February 2000, p. 7.
14. Shelden, p. 233.
15. Greene might even have been tempting Providence. He was a very superstitious novelist and disliked having main characters in his novels whose surname began with the letter 'C': from experience, he

had found this a bad omen (does this relate to his bullying by Carter at school?), and fought against calling the hero of *The Human Factor* 'Castle' for this reason alone, though eventually conceding to his intuition. The name seemed to fit the character, just as he thought that, whatever symbolic associations other critics had read into it, the name 'Lime' for the villain of *The Third Man* seemed apposite to Greene because 'it represented the quicklime in which murderers were said to be buried' (*Ways of Escape*, p. 182). For me, it also seems a gloriously evocative composite of 'Lie' (Harry as the supreme dissembler) and 'slime' (which suggests his natural habitat of the sewers).

16. *A Sort of Life*, p. 141.
17. Sherry, Volume 2, p. 234.

The green baize door

1. *The Lawless Roads*, 1939: London: Penguin Books, 1947, p. 10.
2. *The Power and the Glory*, 1940. London: Heinemann Education edition, 1963, p. 6.
3. From Wordsworth's *Ode: Intimations of Immortality*, Stanza 4.
4. From Greene's review of Basil Wright's documentary film, *Children at School* (1937) in *Night and Day*, 14 October 1937. Greene was obviously very partial to this subversion of Wordsworth, because he uses this phrase at least twice more in the next two years: to evoke Pinkie's rage at the world and readiness for killing at the end of Part Two of *Brighton Rock*; and to describe the hell of his boyhood years in Berkhamsted in the prologue to *The Lawless Roads*.
5. *Collected Essays*, p. 99.
6. Ibid., p. 86.
7. *The Spectator*, 1 May 1936. See Parkinson, p. 97.
8. *Night and Day*, 25 November 1937. See Parkinson, pp. 240–1.
9. See the pamphlet, 'An Interview with Dennis Potter', London: Channel 4 Television, 1994, p. 11.
10. 'The Younger Henry James', *New Statesman and Nation*, 18 July 1953. Published in *Reflections*, selected and introduced by Judith Adamson, London: Reinhardt Books, 1990, p. 154.
11. Ibid., p. 157.
12. Ibid., p. 156.
13. See interview in BBC's 1993 *Arena* documentary.
14. *A Gun for Sale*, Part 1, Chapter 5 (1936: London: Penguin, 1963), p. 124.
15. *A Sort of Life*, p. 25.
16. *A Sort of Newsletter*, Graham Greene Birthplace Trust, Spring 2001, p. 4.
17. *A Sort of Life*, p. 39.
18. *The Other Man*, p. 25.
19. *A Sort of Life*, p. 54. His brother was a senior prefect at the school and therefore part of the 'Establishment'.
20. Ibid., p. 72.
21. *The Lawless Roads*, p. 11.

22. See *The Old School: Essays by Divers Hands*, edited by Graham Greene, London: Jonathan Cape,1934, p. 17.
23. *A Sort of Newsletter*, The Graham Greene Birthplace Trust, Spring 2002, p. 3.
24. *Collected Short Stories*, p. 110.
25. Ibid., p. 103.
26. *The Dangerous Edge*, London: Barrie & Jenkins, 1975, p. 133.
27. *Brighton Rock*, Part 3, Chapter 3, Penguin edition,1970, p. 91.
28. Ibid., end of Part 2, p. 69.
29. Ibid., Part 7, Chapter 9, p. 245.
30. *England Made Me*, London: Penguin Books, 1981, p. 65.
31. *The Human Factor*, London: Bodley Head, 1978, Part 5, Chapter 1, p. 232.
32. *Brighton Rock*, Part 4, Chapter 1, p. 107.
33. See Valentine Cunningham's *British Writers of the Thirties*, Oxford: Oxford University Press, 1989, p. 130.
34. *The Heart of the Matter* (1948: Penguin edition, 1971), p. 50.
35. Ibid., p. 148.
36. Quoted in Alan Ross's book, *Winter Sea*, London: The Harvill Press, 1997, p. 32.

Poets of criminality and conscience: Greene and Hitchcock

1. Raymond Durgnat, *The Strange Case of Alfred Hitchcock*, London: Faber & Faber, 1974, p. 34.
2. See Quentin Falk's *Travels in Greeneland: The Complete Guide to the Cinema of Graham Greene*, Revised and updated third edition, London: Reynolds and Hearn Ltd, 2000, p. 101. Greene is explaining why he refused to sell the film rights of *Our Man in Havana* to Alfred Hitchcock.
3. Ibid., p. 7.
4. I have written about this comparison in *Filming Literature: the Art of Screen Adaptation* (London: Croom Helm, 1986), but even since then, many more parallels have come to light.
5. In Hitchcock's Notebooks, it is said that Greene turned down this opportunity because, after the debacle of *Twenty-one Days*, he had made it a rule only to adapt his own work for the screen. Yet only a few years on, he was to break that rule and adapt Shaw's *Saint Joan* for a film by Otto Preminger.
6. *Hitchcock by Francois Truffaut*, London: Secker & Warburg, 1968, p. 20.
7. See Gene D. Phillips, *Graham Greene: The Films of his Fiction*, New York and London: Teachers' College Press, 1974, p. 85.
8. *A Sort of Life*, p. 29.
9. Peter Conrad, *The Hitchcock Murders*, London: Faber & Faber, 2000, p. 170.
10. Stephen Wall, 'Aspects of the Novel, 1930–1960' in *The Sphere History of Literature in the English Language, Volume 7*, London: Sphere Books, 1970, p. 229.

11. Durgnat, p. 135.
12. *A Sort of Life*, p. 159.
13. Donald Spoto, *The Dark Side of Genius: The Life of Alfred Hitchcock*, London: Collins, 1983, p. 62.
14. *Hitchcock by Francois Truffaut*, p. 258.
15. See Greene's essay, 'The Last Buchan', written in 1941 and reprinted in *Collected Essays*, London: Bodley Head, 1969, p. 167.
16. *Hitchcock by Francois Truffaut*, p. 75.
17. *The Pleasure Dome*, pp. 1–2.
18. Durgnat, p. 234.
19. Donald Spoto, *The Art of Alfred Hitchcock*, London: W.H. Allen, 1975, pp. 139–43.
20. *A Sort of Life*, p. 213.
21. See David Parkinson's *Mornings in the Dark*, p. 537.
22. *Hitchcock by Francois Truffaut*, p. 266.
23. Ibid., p. 14.
24. Gavin Lambert, *On Cukor*, London: W.H. Allen, p. 129.
25. Peter Wollen, *Signs and Meaning in the Cinema*, London: Thames & Hudson, 1969, p. 115.
26. Leonard Bernstein, *The Unanswered Question*, Cambridge, Mass.: Harvard University Press, 1976, p. 3.
27. Durgnat, p. 136.
28. Edward Thomas 'The Other', ll. 16–20. See *Selected Poems of Edward Thomas*, edited by R.S. Thomas, London: Faber & Faber, 1964, pp. 18–21.

Conclusion: forgotten memories

1. Robert Craft, *Stravinsky: The Chronicle of a Friendship 1948–71*, London: Victor Gollancz, 1972, p. 72. Craft was talking of a dinner engagement at Stephen Spender's, attended by Greene and Stravinsky where, he said, 'conversation-making was very heavy-going'. Greene seemed to Craft very shy, and he seemed to intimidate Stravinsky and his wife (and Stravinsky was not a man who was easy to intimidate). 'They have read all his books, starting with, because of their fascination with Mexico, *The Power and the Glory*,' wrote Craft, 'and they are attracted in advance to the author of them, if not by his obsessions with pity, fear, self-destruction, failure, the need to run away, the hollowness of physical love, the problem of Pelagian moral arguments ... '
2. Paul Theroux, *Picture Palace*, London: Hamish Hamilton, 1978, pp. 18–19.
3. Ibid., p. 30.
4. Greene always claimed to have a poor memory, which he thought a useful attribute for a novelist as it then forced him to invent. This issue came to a curious head at the publication of *The Tenth Man* in 1985, originally a film treatment for MGM in the mid-1940s that Greene had written up in the form of a novel, as was his wont, and, on its rejection by the studio, had since, he claimed, completely forgotten about. As Keith

Waterhouse grumbled in *The Times* (6 September 1984): 'I was struggling over a half-cooked novel when I read that someone had turned up a 60,000 word manuscript that Graham Greene had written years ago and *forgotten about*. I thought briefly about doing away with myself...' (p. 10) Predictably, in *Graham Greene: The Enemy Within*, Michael Shelden was highly sceptical about this story and thought it simply a publicity stunt to boost sales (see pp. 13–14). However, in *The Quest for Graham Greene*, W.J. West says that Greene's papers at Boston College demonstrate that Shelden's dark suspicions are unfounded. 'When he [Greene] was approached for comment by the press with news of the discovery he was completely mystified,' writes West. 'Eventually it was discovered that he had written one of his typical outlines for a film which had never been made. Having identified the project, he still had no memory of having written a publishable text or that he had assigned the publication rights. When he learned that he had and that his treatment was eminently publishable, he gave it the go-ahead and contributed a brief introduction which contained a truthful account of what happened.' (p. 246) Given the sheer volume of Greene's writing, it does not seem to me implausible that an author with a self-confessed weak memory could not remember writing a text he had done forty years previously. It is worth adding that MGM did not go ahead with it probably because of its similarity to a project they were already developing and which did get made, *Desire Me* (1947), starring Greer Garson and Robert Mitchum. This would have been unlikely to jog Greene's memory as it turned out to be one of the biggest flops in the studio's history and the only feature film of MGM's to be released without a director's credit, though George Cukor, Mervyn LeRoy and Jack Conway worked on it at different stages.

5. A detailed list was published in *The Daily Telegraph* on 7 June 1991. The list is reproduced in Anthony Mockler's *Graham Greene: Three Lives, 1904–45*, Arbroath: Hunter Mackay, 1994, p. xiv.
6. Alec Guinness, *My Name Escapes Me*, London: Hamish Hamilton, 1996, p. 118.
7. Cedric Watts, *A Preface to Greene*, London: Pearson Education Ltd, 1997, pp. 82–3.
8. Michael Meyer, *Not Prince Hamlet*, p. 188.
9. Bryan Forbes, *A Divided Life*, p. 217.
10. Ibid.
11. Quoted in Watts, p. 84.
12. I wonder if John Le Carré had that image in mind when he wrote his famous last sentence of *The Spy Who Came in from the Cold?*
13. Shelden, p. 80.
14. See *The End of the Affair*, Book Five, Chapter 2. Penguin edition, 1962, p. 147.
15. E.M. Forster, *Aspects of the Novel* (1927): London: Pelican Books, 1962, p. 34.
16. I have argued this point at greater length in my chapter on David Lean's film of *A Passage to India* in *The Classic Novel: From page to screen*, edited by Robert Giddings and Erica Sheen, Manchester: Manchester University Press, 2000, pp. 147–62.

17. See his 1988 interview with Jay Parini, 'Getting to Know Graham Greene'. Quoted in *Perceptions of Religious Faith in the Work of Graham Greene*, Bern: Peter Lang, 2002, p. 621.

18. Marie-Francois Allain, *The Other Man: Conversations With Graham Greene*, New York: Simon & Shuster, 1983, p. 139.

19. 'Francois Mauriac' (1945) in Graham Greene, *Collected Essays*, London: Penguin Books, 1970, p. 92.

20. Ibid.

21. Ibid., p. 93.

22. David Lodge expressed this wittily in *The Language of Fiction* when he suggested that a problem with Virginia Woolf's method was that her characters might have thoughts about eternity whilst peeling potatoes but they never had thoughts about peeling potatoes.

23. Although he was never a very musical man, Greene did once mention to Christopher Hawtree that he quite liked Mahler (*Sunday Telegraph*, 12 April 1998, p. 3). As well as their religious torments, he and Mahler shared a suspicion of unlined faces that were not yet marked by experience. Mahler felt this about his young wife Alma (ten years with Mahler were to change all that) as did Greene about Wilson in *The Heart of the Matter* and Pyle in *The Quiet American*. In his essay 'The Experiential God Representations', Roland A. Pierloot makes an evocative and rather beautiful comparison between Sarah's diary in *The End of the Affair* and the 'What God Tells Me' movement that so stunningly concludes Mahler's 3rd Symphony. See *Perceptions of Religious Faith in the Work of Graham Greene*, p. 377.

24. See *Perceptions of Religious Faith in the Work of Graham Greene*, p. 257.

25. The play is set in a brothel in an unspecified city in Central America where the authorities turn a blind eye to corruption. The main action of the play centres on the raid on the house and its subsequent closure. The rights to the play are owned by Bryan Forbes who has made several unsuccessful bids to get the play staged or broadcast by the BBC. It was given a reading at the Graham Greene Festival in Berkhamsted in October 2000. Although the third act seemed underdeveloped, my impression of it overall was of a sympathetic piece, with unusually strong female characters in Greene, and with something of the flavour and atmosphere of Jean Genet's *The Balcony*.

Select Bibliography

Works by Graham Greene

The novels (First British Editions)

The Man Within (London: Heinemann, 1929).
The Name of Action (London: Heinemann, 1930: subsequently suppressed by the author).
Rumour at Nightfall (London: Heinemann, 1931: subsequently suppressed by the author).
Stamboul Train (London: Heinemann, 1932).
It's A Battlefield (London: Heinemann, 1934).
England Made Me (London: Heinemann, 1935).
A Gun for Sale (London: Heinemann, 1936).
Brighton Rock (London: Heinemann, 1938).
The Confidential Agent (London: Heinemann, 1939).
The Power and the Glory (London: Heinemann, 1940).
The Ministry of Fear (London: Heinemann, 1943).
The Heart of the Matter (London: Heinemann, 1948).
The End of the Affair (London: Heinemann, 1951).
Loser Takes All (London: Heinemann, 1955).
The Quiet American (London: Heinemann, 1955).
Our Man in Havana (London: Heinemann, 1958).
A Burnt-Out Case (London: Heinemann, 1961).
The Comedians (London: Bodley Head, 1966).
Travels With My Aunt (London: Bodley Head, 1969).
The Honorary Consul (London: Bodley Head, 1973).
The Human Factor (London: Bodley Head, 1978).
Doctor Fischer of Geneva or The Bomb Party (London: Bodley Head, 1980).
Monsignor Quixote (London: Bodley Head, 1982).
The Tenth Man (London: Bodley Head and Anthony Blond, 1985).
The Captain and the Enemy (London: Reinhardt, 1988).

Short stories

The Bear Fell Tree (London: Grayson and Grayson, 1935).
The Basement Room and Other Stories (London: Cresset Press, 1935).
Nineteen Stories (London: Heinemann, 1947).
Twenty-One Stories (London: Heinemann, 1954).
A Sense of Reality (London: Bodley Head, 1963).
May We Borrow Your Husband? And Other Comedies of the Sexual Life (London: Bodley Head, 1967).

Collected Short Stories (London: Bodley Head and Heinemann, 1972).
The Last Word, And Other Stories (London: Reinhardt, 1990).

Stories and screenplays (see also Filmography)

The Future's in the Air (1936).
The Green Cockatoo (1937).
Twenty-One Days (1937).
The New Britain (1940).
Brighton Rock (1947).
The Fallen Idol (1948).
The Third Man (1949).
The Stranger's Hand (1954).
Loser Takes All (1956).
Saint Joan (1957).
Our Man in Havana (1959).
The Comedians (1967).

Poetry

Babbling April (Oxford: Blackwell, 1925).

Plays

The Living Room (London: Heinemann, 1953).
The Potting Shed (London: Heinemann, 1958).
The Complaisant Lover (London: Heinemann, 1959).
Carving A Statue (London: Bodley Head, 1964).
The Return of A.J. Raffles (London: Bodley Head, 1975).
The Great Jowett (London: Bodley Head, 1981).
Yes and No and For Whom the Bell Chimes (London: Bodley Head, 1983).

Travel Books

Journey Without Maps (London: Heinemann, 1936).
The Lawless Roads (London: Longmans, Green, 1939).
In Search of a Character: Two African Journals (London: Bodley Head, 1961).
Getting to know the General (London: Bodley Head, 1984).

Children's Books

The Little Train (London: Eyre & Spottiswoode, 1946).
The Little Fire-Engine (London: Parrish, 1950).
The Little Horse Bus (London: Parrish, 1952).
The Little Steam-roller (London: Parrish, 1953).

Autobiographies

A Sort of Life (London: Bodley Head, 1971).
Ways of Escape (London: Bodley Head, 1980).

Biography

Lord Rochester's Monkey (London: Bodley Head, 1974).

Essays and Criticism

British Dramatists (London: Collins, 1942).
Why Do I Write? (with Elizabeth Bowen and V.S. Pritchett: London: Percival Marshall, 1948).
The Lost Childhood and Other Essays (London: Eyre & Spottiswoode, 1951).
Collected Essays (London: Bodley Head, 1969).
The Pleasure Dome: The Collected Film Criticism (edited by John Russell Taylor: London: Secker & Warburg, 1972).
J'Accuse: The Dark Side of Nice (London: Bodley Head, 1982).
Yours Etc.: Letters to the Press 1945–89 (edited by Christopher Hawtree: London: Reinhardt, 1989).
Why the Epigraph? (London: Nonesuch Press, 1989).
Reflections 1923–1988 (edited by Judith Adamson: London: Reinhardt, 1990).
A World of My Own: A Dream Diary (London: Reinhardt, 1992).
Mornings in the Dark: A Graham Greene Film Reader (edited by David Parkinson: Manchester: Carcanet Press, 1993).

Editor

The Old School: Essays by Divers Hands (London: Jonathan Cape, 1934).
The Best of Saki (London: British Publishers' Guild, 1950).
The Spy's Bedside Book: An Anthology (with Hugh Greene: London: Hart-Davis, 1957).
The Bodley Head Ford Madox Ford (4 volumes: London: Bodley Head, 1962–63).
An Impossible Woman: The Memories of Dottoressa Moor of Capri (London: Bodley Head, 1975).
Victorian Villainies: Four Classic Victorian Tales (with Hugh Greene: Harmondsworth: Viking, 1984).

Contributor

Garbo and the Night Watchmen (edited by Alastair Cook, 1937: London: Secker & Warburg, 1971).
Footnotes to the Film (edited by C. Davy: London: Lovat-Dickinson, 1937).
From Anne to Victoria (edited by Bonamy Dobree: London: Cassell & Co., 1937).
Penguin New Writing (edited by John Lehmann: London, Penguin, 1947).
Alfred Hitchcock's Fireside Book of Suspense (edited by Alfred Hitchcock: New York: Simon & Shuster, 1947).
My Silent War (by Kim Philby: Introduction: London: MacGibbon & Kee, 1968).
Pavilions by the Sea: The Memoirs of a Hotel-Keeper (by Tom Laughton: Introduction: London: Chatto & Windus, 1977).
Night and Day (edited by Christopher Hawtree: London: Chatto & Windus, 1984).
Graham Greene Country (by Paul Hogarth: London: Pavilion Books, 1986).

Works about Graham Greene

Biographies

Sherry, Norman *The Life of Graham Greene: Volume 1, 1904–1939* (London: Jonathan Cape, 1989).

Sherry, Norman *The Life of Graham Greene: Volume 2, 1939–1955* (London: Jonathan Cape, 1994).

Shelden, Michael *Graham Greene: The Enemy Within* (London: Heinemann,1994).

Mockler, Anthony *Graham Greene: Three Lives* (Arbroath: Hunter Mackay, 1994).

West, W.J. *The Quest for Graham Greene* (London: Weidenfeld & Nicholson, 1997).

Cash, William *The Third Woman* (London: Little, Brown & Co., 2000).

Secondary reading

Adamson, Judith *Graham Greene and Cinema* (London: Pilgrim Books, 1984).
Graham Greene: The Dangerous Edge (London: Macmillan, 1990).

Allain, Marie-Francois *The Other Man: Conversations with Graham Greene* (London: Bodley Head, 1983).

Allen, Walter *The Modern Novel* (London: Dutton, 1965).

Allott, Kenneth and Farris, Miriam *The Art of Graham Greene* (London: Hamilton Press, 1951).

Annakin, Ken *So You Wanna be a Director?* (Sheffield: Tomahawk Press, 2001).

Atkins, John *Graham Greene* (London: Calder, 1957).

Bergler, Edmund *The Writer and Psychanalysis* (Madison, Connecticut: International Universities Press, 1950).

Bergonzi, Bernard *Reading the Thirties* (London: Macmillan, 1978).

Bowen, Marjorie *The Viper of Milan* (London, 1906: republished: Harmondsworth: Peacock, 1963).

Carey, John *The Intellectuals and the Masses* (London: Faber, 1992).

Chaplin, Charles *My Autobiography* (London: Bodley Head, 1964).

Conrad, Peter *The Hitchcock Murders* (London: Faber & Faber, 2000).

Couto, Maria *Graham Greene: On the Frontier* (London: Macmillan, 1988).

Craft, Robert *Stravinsky: The Chronicle of a Friendship 1948–1971* (London: Victor Gollancz, 1972).

Cunningham, Valentine *British Writers of the Thirties* (Oxford: Oxford University Press, 1989).

Drazin, Charles *In Search of the Third Man* (London: Andre Deutsch, 1999).

Duran, Leopoldo *Graham Greene: Friend and Brother* (London: Harper Collins, 1994).

Durgnat, Raymond *The Strange Case of Alfred Hitchcock* (London: Faber, 1974).

Falk, Quentin *Travels in Greeneland: The Complete Guide to the Cinema of Graham Greene* (3rd edition: London: Reynolds & Hearn, 2000).

Forbes, Bryan *A Divided Life* (London: Heinemann, 1992).

Guinness, Alec *Blessings in Disguise* (London: Hamish Hamilton, 1985). *My Name Escapes Me* (London: Hamish Hamilton, 1996).

Hazzard, Shirley *Graham Greene on Capri* (London: Virago, 2000).

Hellman, Lillian *Pentimento* (London: Quartet Books, 1976).
Hill, Wm. Thomas (ed.) *Perceptions of Religious Faith in the Work of Graham Greene* (Bern: Peter Lang, 2000).
Hynes, Samuel (ed.) *Graham Greene: A Collection of Critical Essays* (New York: Prentice-Hall, 1973).
Kelly, Richard *Graham Greene* (New York: Frederick Ungar, 1984).
Korda, Michael *Charmed Lives* (London: Penguin, 1980).
Lambert, Gavin *The Dangerous Edge* (London: Barrie & Jenkins, 1975).
Lodge, David *The Art of Fiction* (London: Penguin, 1997).
McQueeney, Maire *The Brighton Rock Picture Book* (Brighton: Dining Table Publications Ltd, 1999).
Meyer, Michael *Not Prince Hamlet: Literary and Theatrical Memoirs* (London: Secker & Warburg, 1989).
Meyers, Jeffrey (ed.) *Graham Greene: A Revaluation* (New York: St Martin's Press, 1990).
Miller, R.W. *Understanding Graham Greene* (Carolina: University of Carolina Press, 1990).
O'Connor, Garry *Ralph Richardson* (London: Hodder & Stoughton, 1982).
O'Connor, William Van (ed.) *Forms of Modern Fiction* (Minnesota: University of Minnesota Press, 1948).
O'Prey, Paul *A Reader's Guide to Graham Greene* (London: Thames & Hudson, 1988).
Orwell, George *Collected Essays* (London: Secker & Warburg, 1961).
Pendleton, Robert *Graham Greene's Conradian Masterplot* (New York: St Martin's Press, 1996).
Phillips, Gene D. *Graham Greene: The Films of His Fiction* (New York: Teachers' College Press, 1974).
Pryce-Jones, David *Graham Greene* (Edinburgh: Oliver & Boyd, 1963).
Ross, Alan *Winter Sea* (London: The Harvill Press, 1997).
Sharrock, Roger *Saints, Sinners, Comedians: The Novels of Graham Greene* (Tunbridge Wells: Burns & Oates, 1984).
Smith, Grahame *The Achievement of Graham Greene* (London: Harvester, 1986).
Spoto, Donald *The Art of Alfred Hitchcock* (London: W.H. Allen, 1975).
Spurling, John *Graham Greene* (London: Methuen, 1983).
Stratford, Philip *Faith and Fiction* (Indiana: University of Notre Dame Press, 1964).
Theroux, Paul *Picture Palace* (London: Hamish Hamilton, 1978).
Tynan, Kenneth *Curtains* (London: Longmans, 1961). *Profiles* (London: Nick Hern Books, 1989).
Watts, Cedric *A Preface to Graham Greene* (London: Pearson Education, 1997).
Wobbe, R.A. *Graham Greene: A Bibliography and Guide to Research* (New York: Garland, 1979).
Woodman, Thomas *Faithful Fictions: The Catholic Novel in British Literature* (Milton Keynes: Open University Press, 1991).
Wyndham, Francis *Graham Greene* (London: Longmans, 1955).

Filmography

1934: *Orient Express* (dir.: Paul Martin)
Screenplay: Paul Martin, William Conselman, Carl Hovey, Oscar Levant. Based on the novel *Stamboul Train*.
Leading actors: Heather Angel, Norman Foster, Ralph Morgan, Una O'Connor.

Greene saw this film in Tenerife on his way to Liberia and records the experience in *Journey without Maps*: 'It was a bad film, one of the worst I have ever seen; the direction was incompetent, the photography undistinguished, the story sentimental. If there was any truth in the original it had been carefully altered, if anything was left unchanged it was because it was untrue. By what was unchanged I could judge and condemn my own novel...'

1937: *The Green Cockatoo* Aka: *Four Dark Hours* or *Race Gang* (dir.: William Cameron Menzies)
Screenplay: Edward O. Berkman, Arthur Wimperis. Based on a Greene story and scenario. *Music*: Miklos Rozsa. *Photography*: Mutz Greenbaum (Max Greene).
Leading actors: John Mills, Rene Ray, Robert Newton, Bruce Seton.

1937: *The Future's in the Air* (dir.: Alex Shaw)
Producer: Paul Rotha for Strand Film Company
Commentary written by Greene. *Music*: William Alwyn. *Photography*: George Noble.

1937: *Twenty-One Days* (dir.: Basil Dean)
Screenplay: Graham Greene and Basil Dean. From the short story 'The First and the Last' by John Galsworthy. *Music*: John Greenwood. *Photography*: Jan Stallich.
Leading actors: Laurence Olivier, Vivien Leigh, Leslie Banks, Francis L. Sullivan, Hay Petrie, Robert Newton.
Film not released until 1940.

A barrister's brother accidentally kills a man and allows a down-and-out to take the blame. The characterisation has the whiff of authentic Greenery, particularly the spiritual masochism of the wrongly accused; and Hay Petrie's minister of religion now reduced to beggary and victimisation is a powerful characterisation. Laurence Olivier's flamboyance (which sometimes gives him the appearance of a young James Cagney) is somewhat excessive, and Vivien Leigh just looks bemused. Greene was scathing about the pedantry of his director, but it is not badly done: there is a neat mirror shot when the bad brother turns up in the good brother's chambers, like a shadow across what

Charles Lamb would have called his 'noontide of prosperity'; and there is a sharply observed dinner scene when a group of lawyers jokingly recall incidents where they have broken the law. Within the melodramatic contrivances of the material, there are some emergent Greene themes – social injustice, class division, the pressure of guilt, the compulsion to confession. Even fate takes a hand. A carefree young lover walks blithely under a ladder as if tempting providence: it will be the last carefree moment for Twenty-One Days. Holly Martins will do the same thing in *The Third Man*, and his future progress will be jinxed also.

1940: *The New Britain* (dir.: Ralph Keene)
Commentary written by Graham Greene
1942: *This Gun for Hire* (dir.: Frank Tuttle)
Screenplay: Albert Maltz, W.R. Burnett From the novel *A Gun for Sale*.
Music: David Buttolph. *Photography*: John Seitz.
Leading actors: Alan Ladd, Veronica Lake, Robert Preston, Laird Cregar, Tully Marshall, Marc Lawrence.

A tight little film noir, superbly photographed by the great John Seitz who was the cameraman on Billy Wilder's *Double Indemnity* and *Sunset Boulevard*. Whereas Greene's novel was set in Nottingham in the 1930s and alluded to the contemporary political scene in England and Europe, this Hollywood version transposes the action to Los Angeles in the early 1940s and deals with Fifth Columnists in post-Pearl Harbor America. Its most striking feature is its characterisation of the professional gunman Raven, who murders two innocent people in the first few minutes but spares a crippled child on the stairway out of a haunted recognition, we will deduce later, of his own crippled childhood. Like Pinkie, this baby-faced killer carries scars of both a physical and psychological kind but is humanised through remembrance of a tormented youth and through the good auspices of a young woman who senses the pain behind the bravado and brutality. Alan Ladd and Veronica Lake gave charismatic, star-making performances and there are even anticipations of *The Third Man* in Raven's fondness (like Lime's) for cats and an underground chase, which is here located in an old gasworks. Two fine writers, W.R. Burnett (author of *Little Caesar* and *High Sierra*) and Albert Maltz (later to become one of the Hollywood Ten) give the dialogue an authentic noir tartness, as in an exchange when one of the characters is asked, 'How would you like $5000 – dead or alive?' to which he replies philosophically: 'Wouldn't care for it dead.' This tale of betrayal and double-cross is smartly directed by Frank Tuttle, who was later to betray Jules Dassin and others and name names to the House UnAmerican Activities Committee during the McCarthy witch-hunt.

1942: *Went the Day Well?* US title: *Forty-Eight Hours* (dir.: Alberto Cavalcanti)
Screenplay: John Dighton, Diana Morgan, Angus MacPhail From the Greene short story 'The Lieutenant Died Last'. *Music*: William Walton. *Photography*: Wilkie Cooper.

Leading actors: Leslie Banks, Elizabeth Allan, Basil Sydney, Valerie Taylor, Mervyn Johns, Marie Lohr, David Farrar, Thora Hird, Harry Fowler.

A 'What if...?' parable of great force. The film speculates on the impact of a German takeover of an English village in wartime, an invasion aided by the village squire who is a quisling. James Agee wrote perceptively of the film's atmosphere of an 'Auden prophecy come true', perhaps thinking of a poem like Auden's unnerving 1932 ballad 'O what is that sound?' where the forces of militarism come ever nearer and are finally at one's very door. The film powerfully dramatises English solidarity against threat, but it is equally about English complacency (there is a very pointed cut from the Home Guard to a flock of sheep) and the deceptiveness of appearance. Far from being reassuring, it is actually very disquieting: hardly anyone is to be trusted. The violence is sometimes shocking, as 'civilised' people are forced to act quite out of character in an endeavour to expel the nightmare in their midst. This culminates in an extraordinary sequence towards the end where the heroine (beautifully played by Valerie Taylor) has to descend the stairs to shoot the man she loves on realising his treachery, and the use of slow motion conveys a sense of the previously unimaginable being hideously prolonged.

1943: *The Ministry of Fear* (dir.: Fritz Lang)
Screenplay: Seton I. Miller. *Music*: Victor Young. *Photography*: Henry Sharp.
Leading actors: Ray Milland, Marjorie Reynolds, Carl Esmond, Erskine Sanford, Dan Duryea.

The film starts well: the shot of the portentous clock and the man alone in a darkened room has the sense of dread we associate with the vision of this darkest of directors. It then proceeds for a while with an almost Hitchcockian sense of playfulness, abounding in fake fortune tellers, séances, and even a dangerous cake, as a mentally unstable hero discovers that attendance at a charity fete becomes a passport to a world of espionage. There is some quirky detail here, but the frivolity of the narrative development seems sometimes at odds with the intensity of Lang's framing. The cast is undistinguished; the tension drops; the ending disappoints. Yet just as the novel is gaining ground as Greene's most underrated piece of fiction (as indicated by the attention given to it in William Thomas Hill's recent anthology of essays), so too does the film have its champions, most notably David Thomson, who sees in it a formal masterpiece of claustrophobia and confinement that, with its frequent shots of doorways that represent apprehensive entrances to the unknown, gives fear itself a palpable presence and personality. Lang said he fell asleep the last time he attempted to watch the film, but that might have been a prelude to nightmare.

1945: *The Confidential Agent* (dir.: Herman Shumlin)
Screenplay: Robert Buckner. *Music*: Franz Waxman. *Photography*: James Wong Howe.
Leading actors: Charles Boyer, Lauren Bacall, Katina Paxinou, Peter Lorre, George Coulouris, Wanda Hendrix.

Greene's favourite American adaptation of one of his novels, partly because, unlike the British critics, he was enraptured by Lauren Bacall's performance (and in tribute, called the heroine of his unmade film treatment 'Jim Braddon and the War Criminal' by the name of Laureen); and partly because it is not only faithful to his narrative but even gives it a certain logic. Visually it is a bit stolid (Shumlin was essentially a man of the theatre and his only other film was *Watch on the Rhine*) and the pacing is ponderous. I agree with James Agee when he remarked in *The Nation* (10 November 1945) that it could without strain have lost a third of its length. Yet it has an eye for the novel's strange characterisation and its odd humour, with Peter Lorre and George Coulouris in particularly droll form. The suspense grips mainly in the scenes at the guest house, with Katina Paxinou at her most sinister. The political background is intelligently sketched too, retrospectively catching the novel's Orwellian exasperation at English indifference to the Spanish conflict and at its ineffable blindness to the imminence of global conflagration.

1947: *The Man Within* US title: *The Smugglers* (dir.: Bernard Knowles)
Screenplay: Muriel and Sydney Box. *Music*: Clifton Parker. *Photography*: Geoffrey Unsworth.
Leading actors: Michael Redgrave, Jean Kent, Joan Greenwood, Richard Attenborough, Francis L. Sullivan, Felix Aylmer, Ronald Shiner, Ernest Thesiger, Basil Sydney.

1947: *Brighton Rock* US title: *Young Scarface* (dir.: John Boulting)
Screenplay: Graham Greene, Terence Rattigan. *Music*: Hans May. *Photography*: Harry Waxman.
Leading actors: Richard Attenborough, Hermione Baddeley, William Hartnell, Harcourt Williams, Wylie Watson, Nigel Stock, Carol Marsh, Alan Wheatley.

In 1936 Greene wrote an essay for *World Film News* entitled 'The Genius of Peter Lorre' (see Parkinson, pp. 403–4), which particularly paid tribute to Lorre's 'overpowering sense of spiritual corruption'. There is something of that sense in Richard Attenborough's Pinkie here, with his wide-eyed, childlike face, like Lorre, seeming to conceal a mass of unfathomable depravity. This is one of the great examples of British film noir. The murder of Hale in the 'Dante's Inferno' fairground ride is an ingenious elaboration of the novel and powerful Expressionist cinema. One scene could have come straight of Billy Wilder's noir classic, *Double Indemnity* (1944), as a murderer and an unsuspecting, innocent young woman converse tensely whilst the strains of classical music in the background (in this case, Mendelssohn) enclose them in an ironically civilised ambience. The film's controversial ending seems to me to work very well. It chooses not to replicate the darkness of the novel's ending – Greene's 'worst horror of all', surely his homage to Conrad's 'the horror, the horror' – but the irony of the record needle sticking in the groove is cleverly managed and its pause before the full horror of the recorded message discloses itself is genuinely poignant. It is not God's mercy that has caused the needle to stick on Pinkie's 'I love you', but Pinkie himself, who has damaged the record in trying to smash It earlier: yet another of his plans that has backfired. It does not really sentimentalise the ending since, as Greene said, Rose would be bound to move the needle forward eventually, but the effect is to leave the film in a temporarily merciful limbo rather than plunging you inexorably towards a private hell. It is a very filmic ending too: visually concentrated, perfectly timed, and with an eloquent soundtrack, in which the repetitive click after Pinkie's toneless declaration of love gives the impression of the words sticking in his throat.

1947: *The Fugitive* (dir.: John Ford)
Screenplay: Dudley Nichols From the novel *The Power and the Glory*.
Music: Richard Hageman. *Photography*: Gabriel Figueroa.
Leading actors: Henry Fonda, Dolores del Rio, Pedro Armendariz, J. Carroll Naish, Ward Bond, John Qualen.

This tells you more about the certainties of John Ford's Catholicism than the doubts of Graham Greene's, which in turn diminishes the tale's narrative energy and tension. Greene's fallible priest has been whitewashed (the illegitimate child has here been fathered by the Chief of Police) and Henry Fonda's somnambulistic performance exudes not human complexity but devitalised nobility. Almost like Hitchcock's *I Confess* in its self-revealing piety and often sunk by Richard Hageman's insistent score, the film is a simple statement of faith and a stylised allegory of dignity in suffering and persecution in a totalitarian state. Whilst dramatically dead, it is beautifully photographed by Gabriel Figueroa (Buñuel's regular cameraman).Visually the film is a veritable poem of light and shadow, to suggest the complex shadings of good and evil in the human heart that are particularly reflected here in three finely ambivalent performances – Pedro Armendariz's Police Chief, Ward Bond's murderer, and J. Carroll Naish's betrayer, characters all deeply divided against themselves.

1948: *The Fallen Idol* (dir.: Carol Reed)
Screenplay: Graham Greene Based on his short story 'The Basement Room'.
Music: William Alwyn. *Photography*: Georges Perinal.
Leading actors: Ralph Richardson, Michele Morgan, Bobby Henrey, Sonia Dresdel, Dora Bryan, Denis O'Dea, Jack Hawkins, Walter Fitzgerald, Bernard Lee, Geoffrey Keen, George Woodbridge, Dandy Nichols.

Greene's first collaboration with Carol Reed secured him his one and only Oscar nomination for best screenplay. Greene always expressed a preference for this film over *The Third Man*, because, he said, this was more of a writer's film whereas the latter was more of a director's. By shifting the location and changing the tone of the original story, he created almost a new work, and certainly one of his most engaging. A lot of the characteristic themes and images are there, though: childhood as a foreign country; adult corruption undermined by lethal innocence; and a game of hide-and-seek in the dark – one of Greene's childhood favourites – which inadvertently summons up spectres of sexual jealousy and anguish from out of the shadows.

1949: *The Third Man* (dir.: Carol Reed)
Screenplay: Graham Greene. *Music*: Anton Karas. *Photography*: Robert Krasker.
Leading actors: Joseph Cotten, Alida Valli, Trevor Howard, Orson Welles, Bernard Lee, Ernst Deutsch, Siegfried Breuer, Erich Pontu, Wilfred Hyde-White.

1953: *The Heart of the Matter* (dir.: George More O'Ferrall)
Screenplay: Ian Dalrymple, Lesley Storm. *Photography*: Jack Hildyard.
Leading actors: Trevor Howard, Elizabeth Allan, Maria Schell, Peter Finch, Denholm Elliott, George Coulouris, Gérard Oury, Earl Cameron, Michael Hordern.

Apart from the ending (the act of suicide is evaded, though the intention is clearly signalled), this is generally a faithful rendition of the novel's religious anguish. Sympathetically cast throughout, the film is dominated by a magnificent performance by Trevor Howard, an actor who can be almost as eloquent with his forehead as with his voice to convey the pressure of emotion. As 'Scobie the Just', he embodies the torment of a proud man entangled in an emotional situation too powerful for him to unravel or escape from. The direction is discreet more than terribly imaginative, but the local colour is not overdone and the film skilfully gets across Green's masterful ability to combine complex morality and narrative propulsion in a tense coexistence. As the temptation of suicide draws closer, great visual prominence is given to the image of the revolver in the drawer, and one's mind flits yet again to Greene's 'Russian Roulette' episode in 'The Revolver in the Corner Cupboard'. Curious how often this motif – a revolver unexpectedly in the hand of someone who could never have expected nor desired to be the carrier of such potential violence – recurs in Greene's work: it will happen too, for example, in *Went the Day Well?*, *Brighton Rock*, *The Third Man*, *The Stranger's Hand* and *Our Man in Havana*. In fiction as in life, he did enjoy playing with fire.

1954: *The Stranger's Hand* (dir.: Mario Soldati)
Screenplay: Guy Elmes From an original story by Graham Greene (who also co-produced). *Music*: Nino Rota. *Photography*: Enzo Serafin.
Leading actors: Richard O'Sullivan, Trevor Howard, Alida Valli, Richard Basehart, Eduardo Ciannelli, Stephen Murray.

The startingpoint for this film was an elaboration of a Greene paragraph he had written for a *New Statesman* literary competition to write in the style of Graham Greene and in which he came only second. A schoolboy is due to meet his father in Venice, only to discover that he has been kidnapped. It has the ambience of *The Third Man* (an evocative foreign setting) and the situation of *The Fallen Idol* (the child in a hostile adult world) but lacks the coherence and grip of either. As with many films of Greene, one is struck by the babble of foreign languages, as if he saw this as some existential state of mind (man adrift in a universe whose language he does not understand); and the child's loneliness and the doctor's anguish are sympathetically conveyed. But despite a good cast, the weak direction prevents the material from ever coming to life. It is never entirely clear why the father (Trevor Howard) has been kidnapped in the first place. To play drugged or comatose for much of the time might have suited Trevor Howard's social arrangements, but it does not make for dynamic drama.

1955: *The End of the Affair* (dir.: Edward Dmytryk)
Screenplay: Lenore Coffee. *Music*: Benjamin Frankel. *Photography*: Wilkie Cooper.
Leading actors: Deborah Kerr, Van Johnson, Peter Cushing, John Mills, Stephen Murray, Michael Goodliffe.

In his book, *The Third Woman*, William Cash dismissed this film as 'so abysmal, partly as a result of the moral censorship, that when its director Edward Dymtryk – one of the so-called Hollywood 10, jailed for contempt of Congress after refusing to confirm his former Communist sympathies – died in July 1999, many of his lengthy newspaper obituaries did not even bother to mention it.' This contrasts with Graham Greene's own description of it in a rare surge of enthusiasm as the 'least unsatisfactory' of the film versions of his religious novels.

The film was made at Shepperton Studios in 1954 and released the following year. Greene visited the set and his one abiding memory of the occasion was of watching a love scene between Van Johnson and Deborah Kerr, where Johnson would put some chewing gum in his mouth when the camera was on her but would remove it when it was on him. The original preference for the role of Bendrix had been Gregory Peck who, however, wanted Greene to adapt his novel. In the event, they got Van Johnson and the novel was adapted by Lenore Coffee, a specialist in writing melodramas about women in torment (she had scripted Bette Davis movies such as *The Great Lie*, *Old Acquaintance* and *Beyond the Forest* and more recently a fine thriller, *Sudden Fear* for that mistress of masochism, Joan Crawford). In other words, she was very good on emotionally unfulfilled women struggling with boring husbands or neurotic/psychopathic lovers, or both. This might explain why the role of Sarah registers so strongly. Elsewhere the adaptation simplifies the novel's structure and, for the sake of credibility, reduces the number of miracles. Dymytryk felt that the central dramatic point was Sarah's belief that her prayer had brought Bendrix back to life.

I feel Cash might have missed the point about Dmytryk. Although the director did indeed fall foul of the House of UnAmerican Activities Committee, a salient fact is that he was the only one of the Hollywood 10 who subsequently recanted and named names for the Committee, which allowed him to be reinstated and his career to resume. This may have given him some insight into Sarah's anguish and conflict of loyalties in *The End of the Affair*. The themes of guilt, betrayal, trust (a key word in the film), of loyalty to a cause or creed in conflict with loyalty to one's friends or loved ones, figure strongly. (During the time he was on the blacklist, his first wife committed suicide.) Also his film noir background, on 40s films such as *Farewell My Lovely* and *Crossfire*, can be seen here in the atmospheric use of light and shadow and the use of mirror shots in the early scenes between Bendrix and

Sarah which are often a film noir signifier of deception (Sarah has a shadow side that the hero fails to see). The film is visually striking on occasions. After her prayer has been 'miraculously' answered, Sarah walks out into the street amongst the wreckage of the bombing: the setting suddenly seems a highly charged objective correlative to her state of mind – her sense of confusion, fragmentation, need to rebuild. There is a finely conceived scene near the end where dramatic moments in an upstairs bedroom are implied by the trembling of a chandelier in the room beneath, and the climax reached when it suddenly goes still.

If Quentin Falk was reminded of David Lean's 1945 classic, *Brief Encounter*, I think this is partly to do with Benjamin Frankel's music, with its strong piano theme; partly to do with the 'eternal triangle' situation; but particularly to do with one scene where the heroine, like Celia Johnson in *Brief Encounter*, becomes unexpectedly emotionally distraught and the husband tries to deal with it, and where the way he deals with it is somehow part of the problem. Fred in *Brief Encounter* says 'you can help me with *The Times* crossword puzzle' and Henry in this film offers the proverbial cup of tea. So kind, so reasonable: yet it is this combination of decency and dullness that becomes so stifling to the women. Peter Cushing as Henry is extremely good: a bit prissy and pathetic but at odd moments suddenly sensitive and vulnerable – a paradigm of what E.M. Forster was to call the 'undeveloped hearts' of the English middle class where kindness substitutes for real passion. Van Johnson remains a problem, so wooden a performer that you never know what she sees in him. He was never the liveliest of actors: he could not even enjoy himself in Brigadoon let alone during the Blitz. Evelyn Waugh did not like it much ('the heroine alone was moving'), but he did remark that 'oddly enough, she and the hero had at moments the look of Catherine and Graham'. Within its own terms the film is a compelling exploration of the tension between sacred and profane love; and nobody at that time (or since?) could surpass Deborah Kerr in exposing the raw repression lurking beneath the surface of the English rose.

1956: *Loser Takes All* (dir.: Ken Annakin)
Screenplay: Graham Greene. *Music*: Alessandro Cicognini. *Photography*: Georges Perinal.
Leading actors: Rossano Brazzi, Glynis Johns, Robert Morley.

Ken Annakin's autobiography *So You Wanna Be A Director* offers an amusing account of working with Greene on this film. As he often did, Greene wanted Trevor Howard to play his hero: indeed, according to screenwriter Guy Elmes, he would like to have *been* Trevor Howard, the 'near gent combined with man-of-action' for whom the one enemy was boredom (see Falk, p. 77). He also wanted Orson Welles to play the Korda-like tycoon. Annakin agreed, and suggested Audrey Hepburn for the female lead. In the event they had to make do with Rossano Brazzi, Robert Morley and Glynis Johns. Greene's screenplay contrives some nice aphorisms for Morley, such as his comment on wives: 'Life can be very peaceful without them.' However, he is unwise enough to put into Brazzi's mouth a sentiment shared by many of the film's audience: 'I've had enough of this nonsense.' It is one of Greene's most underdeveloped stories, and a 1990 remake directed by James Scott, who had made a superb short film of *A Shocking Accident*, fared no better. Annakin thought the failure of the film was due to 'wrong casting' and the novel's topsy-turvy moral standpoints, which he felt puzzled and alienated audiences.

Interestingly, Annakin was later to meet Korda, whom Greene had satirised in his novel. Korda bore no malice and indeed offered his own view of why Greene is so difficult to adapt for the screen. 'If you were seeking a big commercial success,' he told Annakin, 'it would never come with a Graham Greene satire. He's almost a genius, but sometimes too clever – clever for the average cinema audience.' It might sound a bit glib, but is it not a shrewd prediction of the fate that would later befall such promising projects as Carol Reed's *Our Man in Havana* and George Cukor's *Travels With My Aunt?*

1957: *Saint Joan* (dir.: Otto Preminger)
Screenplay: Graham Greene From the play by George Bernard Shaw.
Music: Mischa Spoliansky. *Photography*: Georges Perinal.
Leading actors: Jean Seberg, Richard Widmark, Richard Todd, Felix Aylmer, Finlay Currie, John Gielgud, Anton Walbrook, Harry Andrews, Barry Jones, Bernard Miles.

1957: *Across the Bridge* (dir.: Ken Annakin)
Screenplay: Guy Elmes and Denis Freeman. Based on the Greene short story
Music: James Bernard. *Photography*: Reginald Wyer.
Leading actors: Rod Steiger, David Knight, Marla Landi, Noel Willman, Bernard Lee, Bill Nagy, Eric Pohlmann.

This was a personal favourite of Rod Steiger; is regarded as a masterpiece by Mike Leigh; and figures on the Top Ten List of Quentin Tarantino. It bears out Greene's own contention that the best adaptations are often based on short stories rather than novels, because these allow for imaginative expansion of the original rather than contraction. What is remarkable about Guy Elmes's adaptation (which benefited from the consultation and endorsement of Greene's great friend, John Stafford) is that his enlargement seems so true to the spirit of Greene's work, with its complicated and convoluted plotting, the mishmash of languages, the sensitivity to place, the theme of crossing borders. In some ways the film seems closer to the atmosphere of Greene's *The Power and the Glory* – the story was written about the same time – than any film version yet made of that novel. Rod Steiger's towering performance of a tormented and reviled outsider, whom everyone tries to trap and who finally betrays himself through a perverse act of love for his dog, is perhaps the definitive portrayal of that potent Greene archetype – the hunted man at the end of his tether. It is a work like no other British film of the time and even anticipatory of Orson Welles's *noir* masterpiece *Touch of Evil* a year later.

1957: *Short Cut to Hell* (dir.: James Cagney)
Screenplay: Ted Berkeman, Raphael Blau, W.R. Burnett, Albert Maltz. Based on

A Gun for Sale (and the screenplay for *This Gun for Hire*)
Music: Irvin Colbert. *Photography*: Haskell Boggs.
Leading actors: Robert Ivers, Georgann Johnson, William Bishop.

This has little to do with Greene and is of interest mainly for being James Cagney's one and only film as a director, a job he did not enjoy. 'Directing I find a bore,' he wrote in his autobiography (the film bears this out). 'I have no interest in telling other people their business.' A great title for a Graham Greene piece, though.

1957: *The Quiet American* (dir.: Joseph L. Mankiewicz)
Screenplay: Joseph L. Mankiewicz. *Music*: Mario Nascimbene. *Photography*: Robert Krasker
Leading actors: Michael Redgrave, Audie Murphy, Claude Dauphin, Georgia Moll, Bruce Cabot.

One of the most curious things about the film versions of his work, Greene always thought, was that the worst films were made by the best directors (i.e. Lang, Ford, Cukor, Preminger, Mankiewicz). He was particularly incensed by this film because he thought – more on the basis of what he had read about it than what he had seen – that Mankiewicz, by making the hero a dupe of the Communists rather than the American, had completely reversed the meaning of his text. However, that is suggesting a political clarity to the ending that this film just does not provide. Moreover it is hard to see the film as a pro-American tract, given the imbalance of sympathies between the two main characters. For all Michael Redgrave's difficulties with his co-star Audie Murphy ('it's one thing to *get* a performance out of an amateur', 'noted Redgrave in his autobiography, *In My Mind's Eye*', 'it's another to give a performance *with* one'), Redgrave's wounded cynicism as the journalist Fowler comes over more sympathetically than the American's seeming innocence and idealism. Indeed, that may be the point. As Pauline Kael noted, the film is about the harm that innocence and crusading idealism can do – not an unprecedented theme in Greene (from *The Fallen Idol* to *A Burnt-Out Case*) and one with a burning contemporary political relevance.

Whereas Greene's novel prophesied American involvement in Vietnam, Mankiewicz's film anticipates a number of war films of the 1980s – *The Year of Living Dangerously* (1982), *Under Fire* (1983), *The Killing Fields* (1984), *Salvador* (1985) – where the leading protagonist is not a combatant but a journalist, who starts just by taking pictures and ends up taking sides. In *The Quiet American* the motivation for that change is really the core of the drama. Controversially perhaps, Mankiewicz does not see the motivation as essentially political. (He once described himself to me as a totally apolitical animal who only voted in elections against people rather than for them.) 'I've often wanted to do a picture about one of those ice-blooded intellectuals,' he said, 'whose intellectualism is really just a mask for completely irrational passion' (see Kenneth L. Geist's *Pictures Will Talk: The Life and Films of Joseph L. Mankiewicz*, New York: Charles

Scribner's Sons, 1978, p. 270). Mankiewicz sometimes saw himself like that, and it is also a description that some have applied to Graham Greene – someone whose ostensibly intellectual motives may be driven by hidden passions, and who might act politically but for emotional reasons. The film's ending may not be the novel's, but, because of Redgrave's magnificent performance of a troubled soul yearning for forgiveness and redemption, it still packs a punch.

If Greene disliked it, the film found a combative champion who was quick to label Mankiewicz the 'most intelligent man in all cinema' and thought the film a 100% improvement on the novel: namely, Jean-Juc Godard. 'Such delicacy in the scenario, so many gems in the dialogue,' he wrote (see *Godard on Godard*, London: Secker & Warburg, 1972, pp. 81–4). 'All that is missing is cinema.' He thought it the best film of 1958 – quite a claim in the year of *Vertigo*, *Wild Srawberries* and *Touch of Evil*. For lovers of Mankiewicz's work, all the trademarks are there – the theme of betrayal, the eloquent use of flash-back, and a wit which is, in places, sharper than the novelist's. When Fowler asks for a cigarette and the American offers him the whole pack, Fowler snaps back testily: 'I asked for one cigarette, not economic aid!'

1959: *Our Man in Havana* (dir.: Carol Reed)
Screenplay: Graham Greene. *Music*: Hermanos Deniz. *Photography*: Oswald Morris.
Leading actors: Alec Guinness, Burl Ives, Ernie Kovacs, Maureen O'Hara, Jo Morrow, Noel Coward, Ralph Richardson, Paul Rogers.

1961: *The Power and the Glory* (US tv movie: dir.: Marc Daniels)
Screenplay: Dale Wasserman. *Music*: Laurence Rosenthal. *Photography*: Alan Posage, Leo Farrenkopf.
Leading actors: Laurence Olivier, George C. Scott, Julie Harris, Mildred Natwick, Martin Gabel, Cyril Cusack.

1967: *The Comedians* (dir.: Peter Glenville)
Screenplay: Graham Greene. *Music*: Laurence Rosenthal. *Photography*: Henri Decae.
Leading actors: Richard Burton, Elizabeth Taylor, Alec Guinness, Peter Ustinov, Paul Ford, Lillian Gish, James Earl Jones, Raymond St Jacques, Cicely Tyson, Roscoe Lee Browne.

This is a generally dull film, with a hideous performance from Elizabeth Taylor and a rather delicate and undervalued one from Peter Ustinov as her cuckolded husband. It is worth sitting through for a magical scene towards the end when, on the run and in a dimly lit cemetery, Brown (Richard Burton) and Jones (Alec Guinness) sit upon the ground and tell sad stories of the death of their illusions. The scene is mainly Guinness's, drawing every last drop of humour and compassion from a man unexpectedly disclosing his self-contempt, but he is beautifully supported by the grave, quiet eloquence of Burton's attention. It is a reminder of an aspect of adaptation that Pauline

Kael lauded when she reviewed John Huston's wonderful film of Joyce's *The Dead* (1987) in *The New Yorker* – the joy of performers with faces written on by skill and expertise who can occasionally give you something that cold print cannot quite provide.

1972: *Travels With My Aunt* (dir.: George Cukor)
Screenplay: Jay Presson Allen, Hugh Wheeler. *Music*: Tony Hatch. *Photography*: Douglas Slocombe.
Leading actors: Maggie Smith, Alec McCowen, Lou Gosset, Robert Stephens, Cindy Williams.

Cukor was one of the most stylish and civilised of Hollywood directors and one of its finest directors of actresses, so, on the face of it, he would seem to be ideally cast for this material. 'The warmth and range of both the elderly aunt and her middle-aged nephew attracted me to the story,' he said. He had wanted the part to be played by his great friend Katharine Hepburn, who proved to be unavailable, and at a fairly late stage cast Maggie Smith. It is well known that Greene could only stand watching five minutes of the film on television before switching it off – I suspect after Maggie Smith's first entrance. The film stands or falls on how you respond to the leading perform-ance and it strikes me as one of the most fascinatingly miscalculated pieces of screen acting I have ever seen. Supposedly a life force, the character comes over more like a pantomime dame, and one whose wit is entirely lost through a style of dialogue delivery that takes so long to get to the end of a line that you have forgotten how it began. The *New Yorker* critic, Pauline Kael said of the whole film that 'it seems to run down before it even gets started ... just about everyone in it seems miscast ...' (Certainly the sight and sound of Robert Stephens as Visconti trying to conjure a romantic mood through the crooning of a perfectly dreadful Tony Hatch ballad is a grotesquerie on the scale of Smith's Aunt Augusta.) 'Who knows what kind of private joke Graham Greene was working out in the novel?' asked Kael, which, as we have seen, was a question literary critics asked of it as well, but it was not the private nature of the material that defeated adaptation here: after all, it has worked beautifully on the stage. It just seems laboured and lugubrious. For all the charm of Alec McCowen's performance as the nephew, and indeed of Cindy Williams as the American hippy (the one character who seems to work better in the film than in the novel), Cukor cannot give the serious Greene themes of death and rejuvenation the required comic poignancy that Billy Wilder achieved in his film of the same year, *Avanti!* Even the narrative twist that reveals the real identity of Henry's mother carries much less of a frisson than the similar twist that concluded the grand old Hollywood weepie, *To Each His Own* (1946).

1972: *England Made Me* (dir.: Peter Duffell)
Screenplay: Desmond Cory and Peter Duffell. *Music*: John Scott. *Photography*: Ray Parslow.
Leading actors: Peter Finch, Michael York, Hildegard Neil, Michael Hordern, Joss Ackland, Tessa Wyatt.

One of the guests at the 2001 Graham Greene Festival in Berkhamsted was writer-director Peter Duffell, who gave a very interesting account of adapting *England Made Me* for the screen. The most immediate difference from novel and film is the shift of setting from Sweden to Nazi Germany. There were three reasons for this, Duffell explained: his ignorance about Sweden in the 1930s; the immediate provision of powerful, evocative imagery that an audience would recognise; and the cue given by Greene himself when describing one of the novel's main themes as the growing menace in Europe. At the time of the film's release, this drew inevitable comparisons with Bob Fosse's *Cabaret* (1972), particularly as both feature Michael York as a soft English hero. Yet it seems to me an intelligent change. Greene's novels often take place in a context of social and moral hysteria, which here not only carries its own expressiveness but highlights an intriguing new theme. In the film, the quiet Englishman, who is equally incapable of complying with or combating the cruel injustices he encounters, becomes an ingenious Thirties' symbol of ineffectual appeasement.

Other changes made were less drastic. Tony's giveaway tie was changed from Harrow to Eton simply because Eton would be more identifiable to an international audience. Tony and Kate were not twins, as in the novel, but siblings, because it was thought that twins are difficult to bring off on film and that casting would have been difficult. Interestingly, one of Duffell's early ideas for the role of Kate, Susannah York might have made that work (coincidentally having the same surname as Michael and a certain physical resemblance), but she turned out already to be committed to a film with Robert Altman, *Images* (1972). I suspect she may not have been attracted to the part anyway, because she had recently appeared in an incestuous drama opposite Peter O'Toole, J. Lee Thompson's *Country Dance* (1969). In the event, the role went to Hildegarde Neil, who gave her finest screen performance in the role. Joss Ackland, who plays Haller in the film, was originally considered for the role of Krogh and is certainly closer to the novel's image of him than Peter Finch, but the film needed a star name. Finch brings authority to the role as well as an ambiguous charisma, creating a man whose attractiveness conceals a cold-blooded, survivor streak. Denholm Elliott was unavailable for the role of Minty, so Duffell went for Michael Hordern, whose scene-stealing perform-ance of sad seediness replicates the way the character upstages everyone else in the novel too.

There is a particularly fine scene between Krogh (Peter Finch) and Haller (Joss Ackland) which is not in the novel and takes place after Krogh's tense meeting with the German Minister. They get out of their car and pace about and, at one stage, Krogh slips and Haller checks his fall (a small but expressive cameo of their relationship). The scene is filmed mainly in long shot against a bare landscape and it was particularly the pictorial value Duffell was after: the sense of people in a physical and moral waste land. It is a fine example of a film-maker seizing on something essential in Greene: the selection of a setting that correlates to states of mind. Elsewhere the film takes few liberties. When adapting Greene, eminent writers may subconsciously feel the need to compete against the original, to rewrite it in their own terms, Duffell felt: a film-maker can be more objective. It is true of this film and also true of Duffell's original script for *The Honorary Consul*. Both remind me of John Huston in the way a keen cinematic intelligence does not attempt to displace a remarkable literary original but is put at its service. 'Pleased enough' was Greene's verdict on the film. From him, this was high praise, and richly deserved.

1973: *La Nuit Americaine* US title: *Day for Night* (dir.: Francois Truffaut)
Screenplay: Francois Truffaut, Jean-Louis Richard, Suzanne Schiffman.
Music: Georges Delerue. *Photography*: Pierre-William Glenn.
Leading actors: Jacqueline Bisset, Jean-Pierre Aumont, Valentina Cortese, Jean-Pierre Léaud, Alexandra Stewart, David Markham, Graham Greene (as Henry Graham).

Shirley Hazzard described Greene's performance in this as 'almost endearingly unconvincing. In a companion scene of the same film, a cat does far better.' This is unfair: Truffaut was a conspicuously good director of cats.

1979: *The Human Factor* (dir.: Otto Preminger)
Screenplay: Tom Stoppard. *Music*: Richard and Gary Logan. *Photography*: Mike Molloy.
Leading actors: Nicol Williamson, Richard Attenborough, Derek Jacobi, Iman, John Gielgud, Robert Morley.

Greene's novel offers a spy thriller almost devoid of action and overt violence, so the weight of the film is thrown onto the performances, the script, and Preminger's cool narrative lucidity. The success of all this is variable. Iman's wholly inadequate performance as Sarah is another addition to that gallery of brief but crucial female figures in Greene film adaptations who are meant to represent the hero's fatal flaw but become instead the film's (one thinks of similar performances in *Our Man in Havana*, *The Honorary Consul*, Mankiewicz's *The Quiet American*). Robert Morley's flabby doctor is a paradoxically light-weight characterisation of someone who should exude an air of heavy menace. Yet Derek Jacobi as the doomed Davis, another man 'contaminated' by love, has a moving vulnerability; Nicol Williamson gives his role as the deceptively dull Castle a bit of colour and complexity; and Richard Attenborough is superb as the security officer Daintry, as baffled by a box of Maltesers as he is by human motive, and who involuntarily builds up a subtle bond of friendship with Castle at precisely the same time as realisation is dawning that he is the traitor in their midst and that they may have 'eliminated' the wrong man. The film's deep financial problems are certainly evident in the film's gathering visual impoverishment but there is an odd kind of expressiveness about this. After all, Greene's novel succeeds not because of its richness of local detail but for its schematic stylisation of intertwining themes of loyalty and treachery in personal as well as political terms. By the end of the film, the shabby set may not persuade you that Castle is stranded on Russian soil but the suggestion is of an isolation and separation that goes beyond a mere question of place: the drab landscape is not that of Moscow but that of the mind.

1982: *A Shocking Accident* (dir.: James Scott)
Screenplay: James Scott, Ernie Eban. *Music*: Simon Brint, Simon Wallace.
Photography: Adam Barker-Mill.
Leading actors: Rupert Everett, Jenny Seagrove.

Greene had a thing about pigs. He often dreamt about them. He also wrote about them. In 1934, shortly after seeing Walt Disney's famous 1933 cartoon, *Three Little Pigs*, he wrote an article entitled 'The British Pig' where he argues that the pig as an animal has a lot of endearingly British qualities: honesty, slight stupidity, modest commercial sense, idealism. He also praises Beatrix Potter for writing about the love life of pigs with the delicacy of Jane Austen, and offers a sophisticated cultural reading of 'This little piggy went to market.' Many years later, in 1967, he published the short story *A Shocking Accident*, in which a pig plays a major role, falling through a balcony in Italy and crushing the hapless man underneath. But what happened to the pig?

James Scott's film of the tale won the Oscar as best short film of 1982 and is one of the most effective adaptations of a Greene story. It catches the story's sardonic tone but goes a little further. Dealing with a situation of absurd tragedy that has resulted in long-term social embarrassment for the victim's son, the film combines a deadpan humour with a certain sympathy and charm. It shrewdly expands on the original by staging the accident of the title and dramatising those scenes of embarrassment alluded to in the story. It might be that it had a particular resonance for the director. Scott's father was the great painter, William Scott and he was to make a film about him entitled *Every Picture Tells a Story* (1984), in which the most dramatic event is the death of James Scott's grandfather which, curiously enough, was a 'shocking accident': he fell off a ladder during a fire rescue and was killed, an event that haunted his son all his life. The quality of this film might therefore derive from the director's empathy with the material. He feels the sadness beneath the absurdity and can therefore put it across with sincerity as well as sensitivity.

1983: *The Honorary Consul* US title: *Beyond the Limit* (dir.: John Mackenzie)
Screenplay: Christopher Hampton. *Music*: Stanley Myers, Richard Harvey.
Photography: Phil Meheux.
Leading actors: Michael Caine, Richard Gere, Elpidia Carrillo, Bob Hoskins.

Greene felt that the best thing about this film was Michael Caine's poignant performance as the eponymous Consul, Charlie Fortnum, and it would be hard to disagree. Although shrewdly cast to play a man more adept at giving love than accepting it (like his American gigolo), Richard Gere struggles a little to convey Plarr's development from deviousness to decency. Rather like Ernie Kovacs in *Our Man in Havana*, Bob Hoskins misses the menace behind the manners of the policeman. Because of the inadequacy of the actress, the love story does not work at all. The film picks up on some of the important motifs of the novel, notable the insistent theme of 'the father' as seen in both religious and paternal terms, and just occasionally there is a striking visual effect, like the moody shadow that falls across Fortnum's face when he learns of Plarr's betrayal. Generally, however, it misses that intertwining of the political and psychological within the confines of a thriller plot that marks out Greene at his best. Only Caine's performance, particularly in the last ten minutes, conveys some of the dimensions of the novel's moral complexity.

Peter Duffell was originally scheduled to write and direct, but when that arrangement fell through, the task of adaptation was given to Christopher Hampton, no doubt because of the novel's thematic and narrative similarity to Hampton's play, *Savages*. For a creative writer, the joy of adaptation, Hampton told a Greene Festival audience in 2002, is analogous to the kind of joy that Greene described in his *Collected Essays* when talking about reading adventure novels in his childhood: namely, the opportunity it gives for escape into someone else's world. But the studio was always snapping at his heels, grumbling at what they called Gere's 'faggot' (i.e. English) accent, and insisting on a title change when their market research revealed that, of the three words of Greene's title, the only one generally understood was the first.

1984: *Dr Fischer of Geneva* BBC tv film (dir.: Michael Lindsay Hogg)
Screenplay: Richard Broke. *Photography*: Ken Westbury.
Leading actors: James Mason, Alan Bates, Greta Scacchi.

1985: *Monsignor Quixote* Thames tv film (dir.: Rodney Bennett)
Screenplay: Christopher Neame. *Photography*: Norman Langley.
Leading actors: Alec Guinness, Leo McKern, Ian Richardson, Graham Crowden, Maurice Denham.

1986: *May We Borrow Your Husband?* Yorkshire tv film (dir.: Bob Mahoney)
Screenplay: Dirk Bogarde. *Photography*: Peter Jackson.
Leading actors: Dirk Bogarde, Charlotte Attenborough, Francis Matthews, David Yelland, Simon Shepherd.

1988: *The Tenth Man* US tv film (dir.: Jack Gold)
Screenplay: Lee Langley. *Photography*: Alan Hume.
Leading actors: Anthony Hopkins, Kristin Scott Thomas, Derek Jacobi, Cyril Cusack, Brenda Bruce.

1990: *Loser Takes All* US title: *Strike it Rich* (dir.: James Scott)
Screenplay: James Scott. *Music*: Cliff Eidelman, Shirley Walker. *Photography*: Robert Paynter.
Leading actors: Robert Lindsay, Molly Ringwald, John Gielgud, Frances de la Tour, Max Wall.

1999: *The End of the Affair* (dir.: Neil Jordan)
Screenplay: Neil Jordan. *Music*: Michael Nyman. *Photography*: Roger Pratt.
Leading actors: Ralph Fiennes, Julianne Moore, Stephen Rea, Ian Hart, Jason Isaacs.

'It's not what I wrote,' says the novelist Bendrix (Ralph Fiennes) to Sarah (Julianne Moore) when he takes her to see a film version of one of his novels.

It's an in-joke: the film they are watching is *Twenty-One Days*, Greene's debut as a screenwriter which he famously attacked in his other guise as film critic of *The Spectator*. It's an in-joke in another sense too: Jordan's adaptation (which won him a British Academy Award) is not quite what Greene wrote either. The major miscalculation seems to me the resumption of the affair towards the end of the film, which undermines Sarah's sacrifice, sidelines one of the novel's key characters (i.e. God) and is sentimentally rendered. Elsewhere the conflation of the characters, the reduction of the number of miracles and even the transferral of the birthmark from one character to another are done in the spirit of narrative coherence and cohesion and work reasonably well. The period is sharply evoked; the novel's cinematic time-shifts are masterfully negotiated in the editing; and although the casting is controversial (only Ian Hart's 'Parkis is willing' characterisation seemed to me spot-on), the skill of the acting draws one into the drama. It is a film about hearts full of passion, jealousy and hate, as time goes by: not so much shades of Greene perhaps as of *Casablanca*.

In *The New York Review of Books*, Stanley Kauffman described the film as 'a devastation' not 'an adaptation'. 'It's so drastic,' he wrote, 'that we are left puzzled as to why Jordan wanted to adapt the novel at all if he was going to violate it in this way.' It is not as drastic as all that, but, in any case, one could put that the other way around and argue that, if Jordan did not want to change the novel, why make the film? A particular area of interest in the text for him was the extent of love: how far it goes, and where, when and how it ends. 'Love doesn't end just because we don't see each other,' says Sarah. 'The end' becomes a key phrase in the film, as the tale vacillates emotionally between the finite and the infinite, between temporal human existence and the eternity of the sacred. The central dramatic situation also seems to be one that Jordan relishes, as it has occurred in different forms in some of his other works, such as *Mona Lisa* (1986) and *The Crying Game* (1992): namely, the situation of an 'unaffiliated' hero, with no ties or commitments, drawn into and trapped by an impossible love that will be thwarted by an unforeseen obstacle that will wrench control of the relationship out of his grasp.'You'll catch your death,' these people are told, and they stumble in a limbo between life and death. They seem ghostly figures in Purgatory, stalked by guilt, terrified of fading from view but sometimes appearing invisible, empty shells needing to be filled by feeling or faith. It is a war-time story, but the war seems mainly internal; and the atmosphere is dark and dank, as a bleak nightmare unfolds of souls in torment. Nevertheless, as films like *The Company of Wolves* (1984) and *High Spirits* (1988) have shown, Jordan has always had his supernatural side and this is not the first film of his to feature a miracle. For all its faults, there is not a film-maker currently around better qualified to make something challenging and provocative out of this most troubling of novels.

2002: *The Quiet American* (dir.: Phillip Noyce)
Screenplay: Christopher Hampton, Robert Schenkkan.
Music: Craig Armstrong. *Photography*: Christopher Doyle.
Leading actors: Michael Caine, Brendan Fraser, Do Thi Hai Yen.

'I know I'm not essential to her . . . but believe me when I tell you that to lose her will, for me, be the beginning of death.' This is the jaded journalist Fowler talking about his relationship with the beautiful Vietnamese girl Phuong. It is one of the most touching lines in Greene and a reminder that, for all its political ramifications, the novel is a love story – of a man's love not only for a young woman but also for a country. This gives an added piquancy to Fowler's ultimate betrayal of the American, which is a calculatedly political as well as romantic act.

The love triangle is movingly rendered here. Even the three-sided proposal is played straight and has none of the comedy of the novel and indeed of Mankiewicz's film at this point. Fowler's infatuation is important as it explains why he misunderstands for so long the political nature of Pyle's mission: he has been blinded by romantic rivalry. If lacking the neurotic intensity that Michael Redgrave brought to the role, Michael Caine's Fowler is still a fine characterisation, where a predominant languid cynicism can, with the right trigger, give way to impassioned indignation: it is a reminder that Greene put a lot of himself into this character. Do Thi Hai Yen's performance as Phuong is quite luminous, far surpassing the equivalent performance in the 1958 film, and the same can be said for Brendan Fraser's American, who comes on like a Clark Kent innocent but, by his final scene, has revealed a self-righteous and ruthless fanaticism that is truly dangerous.

'It's the American who gives you the trouble,' Christopher Hampton has said about adapting this novel for the screen. The novel's intended contrast between shrewd journalist and naive American is always in danger here of shifting into a conflict between naive journalist and shrewd American. Nevertheless, no harm is done to the essentials. The bomb outrage in the square is properly stunning and shocking, and the novel's prophetic power emphasised by concluding newspaper headlines about the subsequent Vietnam War. The film's release was delayed because of nervousness about its seeming critique of American meddling in a foreign country and the consequences that might follow such politically motivated, precipitate action, but this only underlines the film's topicality, not to mention Greene's continuing, extraordinary relevance as we gingerly assimilate and evaluate today's new world order.

Author Index

Subject Index